How to be British

What they don't teach in
Citizenship Class

William Davis

Illustrations by John Jensen

About the Author

William Davis is an immigrant who came to Britain more than half a century ago and embarked on a highly successful career in the media and business. He is a former financial editor of the *Evening Standard* and the *Guardian*, presenter of the *Money Programme* on television and the *World at One* on radio, and editor of *Punch*. He founded the British Airways inflight magazine, *High Life,* and in the 1990's served as the chairman of the British Tourist Authority and the English Tourist Board.

Other books by William Davis

Three Years Hard Labour

Merger Mania

Money Talks

Have Expenses, Will Travel

It's No Sin To Be Rich

Money in the 1980's

The Rich: a Study of the Species

Fantasy: a Practical Guide to Escapism

The Corporate Infighter's Handbook

The Super Salesman's Handbook

The Innovators

Children of the Rich

The Lucky Generation: a Positive View of the 21st Century

Great Myths of Business

The Alien: an Autobiography

Published by Abingdon Media Services Limited
98 Ebury Mews, London SW1W 9NX

Printed and bound in England by Antony Rowe Limited

ISBN 0-9550410-0-7

Who Are We?

At the first-ever civic ceremony to welcome new citizens, early in 2004, Prince Charles said that even if being British was no longer considered to be the first prize in the lottery of life at least it was "something of a privilege and blessing for us all".

Immigrants who seek to acquire the privilege are expected to take lessons in citizenship (compulsory in schools since 2002) and to pass a test. Successful applicants will have to swear or affirm an oath. It reads:

I swear by Almighty God / do solemnly and truly declare and affirm that, on becoming a British citizen, I will be faithful and bear true allegiance to her Majesty Queen Elizabeth the Second, her Heirs and Successors according to law. I will give my loyalty to the United Kingdom and respect its rights and freedoms. I will uphold its democratic values. I will observe its laws faithfully and fulfil my duties and obligations as a British Citizen.

Newcomers will naturally want to know what those duties and obligations are. The Home Office has published a summary, but there are many unofficial rules that are not on the curriculum and that, judging by their behaviour, many indigenous Brits are not familiar with. Travel guides are inadequate because they tend to focus on what tourists want to see – castles, stately homes, picturesque ruins, Beefeaters, and quaint pageantry.

This book will enlighten you, but the advice it offers need not be taken *too* seriously. We British are fond of irony – a form of humour frequently encountered in the media and our courts of law. It is an attribute you will need to cultivate if you wish to become fully integrated.

You will no doubt have noticed that there is some confusion about what is meant by 'Britishness'. When I first came here as an immigrant, more than half a century ago, this wasn't a problem. It meant taking pride in Britain's historic achievements, traditions, and distinctive culture. People stood up in cinemas when they played the national anthem, sang Rule Britannia at sporting events, and showed respect for the Establishment. Public buildings flew the Union Jack and the possession of a British passport signified that one was special. To be British was to be fair-minded, honest, reticent, polite and tolerant. You also had to believe that the educational system, health service, and other institutions were 'the best in the world'. Any dissent from that comforting perception was seen as evidence that one didn't 'belong'.

Some people feel that nothing much has changed, but it has. When Tony Blair became prime minister in 1997 he declared that there was a 'New Britain' – a 'meritocracy where we break down barriers of class, religion, race and culture'. It sounded good (at least to some of us) but it ignored the obvious fact that Britain was no longer a clearly defined political entity and that many of the barriers remained firmly in place.

The Scots, who have long resented the English habit of muddling up 'England' with 'Britain', now have their own parliament and the Welsh have an Assembly. There is a British National Party, but it is generally held in contempt because of its extremist views and does not have a single seat in the Westminster parliament. There are also numerous organisations with the prefix 'British', including the British Dance Council and the British Arm Wrestling Federation, but some have followed the lead set by the BBC – they use initials because they are less contentious.

Scotland and Wales have increasingly come to see themselves as separate nations. Foreigners often find it puzzling that there is no British team in sports like football and rugby – we cling, more than ever, to the concept that each 'nation' must be represented by its own team and insist that a match between, say, England and Scotland is an 'international event'. (It explains why no-one ever hears a sports crowd shout "Come on Britain").

The English response has been to wave the flag of St George instead of the Union Jack, and even paint it on their faces. Few seem to know, or care, who St George actually was and how he became the patron saint of England. Many would be surprised to learn that he never set foot on English soil and is also the patron saint of Portugal. What matters, to them, is that the flag has become an easily recognisable symbol of Englishness. Some regions argue that they, too, should be given greater autonomy.

Scholars like Norman Davis maintain that 'Britain' is an artificial construct forged together in the 18th century by Protestanism, the Industrial Revolution, and the empire. Many doubt that it will survive if and when there is a United State of Europe. That remains to be seen, but it is certainly reasonable to ask *Who are the British?*

The truth is that we are a complex lot, like all Europeans and possibly even more so, because of our hybrid origins. The Ancient Brits were the first on the scene, followed by the Romans, Normans, Saxons, Scandinavians and others who felt that the islands were attractive enough to put up with the fickle climate. They have been joined, more recently, by immigrants from former colonies and Continental Europe.

A census in 2001 revealed that 4.6 million of us were members of 'ethnic minority groups', out of a total population of 58.7 million. Black and Asian people *born* in Britain, it showed, made up 50 per cent of the country's non-white population for the first time.

More than 120,000 immigrants are granted British citizenship every year. The newcomers who were welcomed so warmly by Prince Charles included people originally from Afghanistan, India, Sri Lanka, Australia, New Zealand, South Africa, Nepal, Poland, Kenya and Somalia.

The official line is that New Britain is a 'multi-cultural society', a label that many of us still find hard to accept. The chairman of the Commission for Racial Equality says that multi-culturalism is out of date and no longer useful, not least because it encourages separateness. He insists that there is 'an urgent need to assert the core of Britishness across society.' Chancellor Gordon Brown, who is widely expected to become prime minister when Tony Blair steps down, agrees. "I believe," he says, "that we have not been explicit enough about what we mean by Britishness for far too long."

This brings us back to the thorny issue of definition. For Brown, a Scot, it's all about 'a passion for liberty, anchored in a sense of duty, and an intrinsic commitment to tolerance and fair play.' Yes, but we can hardly claim that these qualities can only be found in Britain.

It is ironic, you may feel, that many of the people who consider themselves true Brits are immigrants. There is, of course, a simple explanation. 'British' is an inclusive label. We recognise that in order to call oneself English, Scottish, or Welsh, one needs to have been born here. It is easier to be British.

Some of us, however, are just as determined to hold on to our native culture. Parts of England look like a foreign country, with mosques, temples, and numerous sari shops. Foreign influences are also very much in evidence elsewhere, notably London. We eat Chinese noodles and Japanese sushi, drink French and Italian wines, sing Karaoke in bars, dance to Greek and Spanish music, watch American films and TV sitcoms, love curry, and wear lurid Caribbean shirts at the Notting Hill Carnival. There is less enthusiasm for Bavarian lederhosen, sauerkraut, and noisy German beer-hall songs but this is mainly because the war has not yet been forgotten.

Even the English language, far from being a flaunting of national purity, has been affected by massive borrowings from America, Asia, and the Continent of Europe.

We are still said to be a Christian country but that view has been questioned by people like David Hope, until recently the Archbishop of York. He blames 'secularist tendencies' but, of course, there is another reason: many of us are Muslims, Hindus or Jews. Prince Charles says that, if and when he becomes king, he wants to be known as 'defender of all the faiths', not one.

Whether or not this has made Britain better is a matter of opinion. What cannot be denied is that it has had a profound impact on the vaunted British Way of Life.

Some time ago a former Prime Minister, John Major, famously said that "fifty years from now Britain will still be the country of long shadows on county cricket grounds, warm beer, invincible green suburbs, dog lovers – and, as George Orwell said, old maids bicycling to Holy Communion through the morning mist". He was widely mocked because it was plainly a nostalgic view of what England used to be rather than a description of modern Britain. It certainly offended the Scots, who are not mad about cricket and who cherish their own customs – wearing tartan kilts, playing the bagpipes, and eating haggis. Welsh nationalists retain a passionate commitment to their strange language.

The editor of *Prospect*, David Goodhart, maintains that keeping British citizenship special "does not require exclusivity, but if we are to avoid the nasty backlash that grips part of Europe, it does require reassuring existing members that we are taking care about the number and type of people we invite into the club". His view is shared by the Home Office – qualifications include 'not to be of unsound mind' and 'having sufficient knowledge of English, Welsh, or Scottish Gaelic'. The trouble is that citizens of other countries in the European Union have the right to live and work here. They may not want to become British – many don't – but we cannot refuse to let them in. What we are entitled to ask is that everyone should make an effort to understand and accept our codes of conduct, however bizarre or old fashioned they may seem.

History

New citizens are required to know British history but try to avoid sensitive topics like the Norman invasion, the Boer war, and the loss of the British Empire. If you *must* talk about Africa, India, and the Middle East be sure to stress that we made a laudable effort to bring the benefits of civilisation to less fortunate countries and that we withdrew once they were able to govern themselves – a judgement that remains controversial.

It is also bad form to point out that we were driven out of the American colonies by a disloyal rabble and that we failed in our efforts to keep the Suez canal (a best forgotten episode for which the Americans are entirely to blame).

When in Scotland, don't mention Culloden without denouncing the cruel conduct of the English and their German rulers. In England, care must be taken when referring to the War of the Roses, Oliver Cromwell, and other domestic conflicts. Endeavour to find out which side the ancestors of your audience was on before doing so.

You are on safe ground when discussing the defeat of the Spanish Armada, the glorious British victories at Trafalgar and Waterloo, and the heroic stand against the Nazi hordes. Always remind foreigners who won the second world war and resist the temptation to give credit to allies like the Russians. Remember to praise The Few, who made it possible for you to live in Britain without having to worry about jack-booted Nazis knocking on your door at dawn.

You should also be familiar with our success of evicting the Argies from the Falklands. It doesn't matter that the islands are mainly populated by sheep and penguins – uppity foreigners were shown that they had better not mess with us.

Others who discovered this the hard way include Napoleon Bonaparte. In the summer of 1805 he moved an army to Boulogne with the aim of invading Southern England. The emperor looked at the Channel and said: "It's nothing but a ditch". He believed that he needed only 24 hours to begin his conquest. But the Royal Navy blocked the 'ditch' and the French Fleet couldn't get through. He abandoned the invasion. Wellington later thrashed him at Waterloo and he was forced to abdicate.

You *may* be asked about the war of Jenkins's ear. This is a trick question used by some teachers and you are not expected to know the answer. They will be greatly impressed if you do. In 1731, a British captain called Jenkins claimed that he had his ear cut off by the Spanish coastguards when his ship was searched. He was brought before the House of Commons to produce it in a bottle and told MP's: "I commend my soul to God and my cause to my country". It caught the popular imagination and led to angry demands that Spain should be punished. Whether it was in fact his own ear or whether he had lost it in a seaport brawl remains uncertain, but the power of this shrivelled object was immense. The country went to war against the Spaniards some time afterwards and an Englishman wrote a song that is still famous:

When Britain first, at heaven's command,

Arose from out of the azure main,

This was the charter of the land,

and guardian angels sung this strain:

Rule Britannia, rule the waves;

Britons never will be slaves.

But British history is not just about wars. We started the Industrial Revolution and gave the world inventions like the steam engine and the porcelain toilet bowl. Since then Britain has made many other contributions to the welfare of mankind, such as the jet engine, package holidays, the double-decker bus, the queue, and the mini skirt.

Good names to mention in any discussion of history are Francis Drake, Wellington, Marlborough, Isaac Newton, Florence Nightingale, Horatio Nelson, and Winston Churchill. You are also expected to light bonfires in memory of Guy Fawkes, but keep in mind that he was not a hero but what would nowadays be called a terrorist. The fires commemorate his failure to blow up parliament. Cynics think it would have been better if he had succeeded, but as a new citizen you should *never* hint that you share their view.

The Monarchy

Another historical fact that many of us don't like to be reminded of is that our royals are the descendants of German immigrants. Their ancestry dates back from the time when Hanover was a separate kingdom which supplied Britain with a succession of monarchs. Some, like George I, never bothered to learn English. When King George VI as Duke of York married the Lady Elizabeth Bowes-Lyon, the mother of our Queen, he introduced the first drop of British blood into the family for three hundred years. Prince Philip is an immigrant with many foreign relations. The 'House of Hanover' did not become the 'House of Windsor' until the first world war, and even now some English snobs refer to the royals as 'those bloody Germans', though no-one would dare to say that to the Queen, who certainly does not consider herself to be German.

It is important to understand the function of the monarchy – once described by Prince Philip as 'the family firm' – in modern Britain. Her Majesty does not rule: she reigns. (The ruling is done by the occupant of 10 Downing Street). Once a year she puts on her crown and is escorted to the House of Lords, which she enters surrounded by heralds rejoicing in names like the Rouge Dragon Pursuivant, Portcullis Pursuivant, Maltravers Herald Extraordinary, and the Norroy and Ulster King of Arms. Also on hand to greet her are the Earl Marshall and the Lord Great Chamberlain.

Once she is seated on her gilded throne, Black Rod is sent off to 'command' the House of Commons to join the proceedings. The Queen then reads out a speech explaining what her government intends to do next. The speech has been written by the rulers, and she doesn't necessarily agree with their plans. You should not, therefore, assume that she is in any way to blame for unpopular measures.

Reigning involves many other tasks. Her Majesty hosts formal banquets for visiting heads of state, opens hospitals, launches ships, and distributes honours. (It is a common misconception that she decides who should receive them. That, too, is done by the rulers). She is the star attraction at social events like Royal Ascot and at ceremonies like Trooping the Colour, which has its origins in the former custom of parading the colours, or regimental flags, before British soldiers ahead of a battle so they would know which side they were on. This is no longer necessary, but we do not believe in discarding rituals just because they have ceased to be of practical value.

The monarchy is our last stronghold of romantic extravagance, much envied by Americans and the main reason why Britain remains among the world's top tourist destinations. Costumes, drama, music, horses – you name it, the monarchy show has got it. No-one does it better. Most of the cost is met by the state, but the Queen's own lifestyle is not extravagant compared with that of some of her predecessors.

She is a rich woman but her tastes are simple. Lunch and dinner at home are modest affairs because, like all of us, she worries about her figure. One of her favourite pastimes is watching *Eastenders* on television, so she knows how her poorer subjects live. She and the other royals also pay taxes, like everyone else. Her Majesty has several homes, but Buckingham Palace and Windsor Castle do not belong to her. They are owned by us, The People.

She is the head of state in other countries, including Australia and Canada, but always makes a point of showing the world what it means to be British. She gets annoyed when foreigners describe her as 'the Queen of England' (the Scots and Welsh also find it upsetting) and you should *never* do so. A good deal of her free time is spent at Balmoral, the family's place in Scotland, where all the royals habitually gather for Christmas. Her husband, Prince Philip, is also the Duke of Edinburgh and her eldest son wears a kilt when he stalks around the Scottish countryside – a practice which you may find a little confusing because he is Prince of Wales. (Ah, but he is also Lord of the Isles and Great Steward of Scotland: like the Queen, he is determined to show that the monarchy embraces all the nations in what, despite our differences, is still called the United Kingdom).

Your oath requires you to be faithful to her Majesty. This has nothing to do with sexual fidelity: it means that you are not permitted to express greater admiration for other heads of state or to call for the abolition of the monarchy. Bearing 'true allegiance' mainly involves asking God to save her and to be upstanding at banquets when you are requested to raise your glass and join in the loyal toast. ("The Queen", followed by a mumbled "God bless her"). The reference to her 'heirs and successors' is designed to ensure that you do not stray when she takes her rightful place in heaven. If you should meet her before then, which is always a possibility, do not attempt to shake her hand and tell her about your problems. The correct procedure is to wait until she has chosen to speak to you. She should be addressed as "Ma'am" (pronounced Marm) and it will help if you have some knowledge of horses and of corgis, her favourite breed of dogs.

The other royals also expect deferential treatment, but it doesn't have to be excessive. Their role, these days, is less easily defined. They are expected to give their support to various institutions and charities, and to stand in for the Queen when she is too busy to open another hospital, but they are not at all sure what else they are supposed to do. It causes particular anguish to Prince Charles, a kindly man who takes a keen interest in subjects like architecture and farming (he is said to be fond of talking to plants) but who has been subjected to a lot of media criticism since the untimely death of the 'Queen of Hearts', Princess Diana. He is destined to be our future king, and you must show proper respect, regardless of what you have read in newspapers like *The Sun* and the *Daily Mirror*.

The same applies to his new wife. Before their marriage in the spring of 2005 she was plain Mrs Parker-Bowles and his long-tome mistress. (Diana used to call her 'that Rottweiler'). She is now her Royal Highness the Duchess of Cornwall (though legally entitled to call herself the Princess of Wales) and second only to the Queen in the pecking order of royal women. It is planned that this will be changed to Princess Consort when Charles becomes King, but by then the British public may be willing to accept her as Queen. Not bad for the 57 year old daughter of a wine merchant, formerly the wife of a brigadier and Silver-Stick-in-Waiting. The new Duchess is far from regal, but other women are expected to curtsey on greeting her and men will have to bow.

Prince Andrew has done his duty in the armed forces and now tries hard to win foreign contracts for British industry, but he is mainly known for his romantic liaisons. (His marriage to a feisty commoner is considered to have been an unmitigated disaster and the Duchess has since committed the ultimate offence – making commercials for American television). The Princess Royal has a strong commitment to saving the world's children but also shares her mother's love of horses. Prince Edward, who prefers to be known as the earl of Wessex, has tried to make a career in television but it hasn't worked as well as he had hoped.

There is some doubt about the future of the younger generation of 'heirs and successors'. Prince William is second in line to the throne, but will he want the job of king when the time comes? Harry, who is third, has embarrassed the 'family firm' with foolish behaviour – his most notorious stunt was to turn up at a fancy dress party wearing the uniform of Rommel's Afrika Korps complete with a Swastika armband. Dad hopes that officer training at Sandhurst will change him, but it's hard to see Harry in the role of Monarch. (Yes, I know that an earlier Harry – Henry VIII – was worse, but remember that King Charles I had his head chopped off when he insisted that monarchs had a divine right to do what they liked).

There is, inevitably, a great deal of speculation about their girlfriends but they are unlikely to embark on an early marriage. Your daughter may seem an ideal candidate, but their minders would almost certainly object to anyone who doesn't have royal or at least aristocratic blood, however diluted it may be. The princes fully intend to make their own choice, but don't bother to send them a photo of your teenager. It would be bad form and a waste of time.

Free Speech

As a British citizen you are entitled to free speech but make sure that your remarks are politically correct. This can be difficult if you are not familiar with the term – an American import which defines what is acceptable and what isn't. Overstepping the boundaries can get you into trouble. You should avoid saying anything controversial about blacks, Asians, Jews, homosexuals, lesbians, the monarchy, the army, Northern Ireland, feminists, and judges. Acceptable topics are the weather, cars, television sit-coms, and the outrageous attempts by Brussels to interfere with the British way of life.

You are also permitted to join in marches approved by the police but goose-stepping is considered to be un-British. The correct procedure is to saunter along in a disorderly fashion, wearing an anorak or T-shirt. You may carry a poster but it should not contain any statement likely to offend the aforementioned fellow-citizens and institutions. Protesting against government reforms is legal and unusually involves shouting "out! out! out! (New immigrants may prefer to leave this to members of parliament). Muslims are advised to confine themselves to praying in mosques. Marching, shouting, and listening to inflammatory speeches by 'community leaders' is regarded as threatening behaviour and may lead to problems with the authorities.

There are other limits to free speech which you may be aware of. The use of expletives in public is bad form, except at football matches and in pubs.

Many British people are fond of the word 'bloody'. The widespread reliance on this adjective, thought to be relatively harmless, is captured by the following story. Two Yorkshiremen were standing in front of an election poster. "What do they mean", asked one, "by one man one vote?". "Why", says the other, "it means one bloody man, one bloody vote". To which the enquirer replied: "then why the hell don't they bloody well say so".

You may feel that, as a new citizen eager to fit in, you have the right to express yourself in an equally forceful manner. But you run the risk of appearing presumptuous; the safest course is to stick to "goodness gracious" until you are certain that you are genuinely recognised as 'one of us'.

There are also unwritten rules governing the use of hand signals. A common British practise is to use the V-sign, but this can easily lead to blows if you get it wrong. The origin remains something of a mystery. One theory is that the gesture dates back to the Battle of Agincourt. The French, it is said, threatened that they would chop off the index middle finger of every English archer they captured. The archers responded by raising their two fingers whenever they managed to shoot a French soldier – defiantly showing that they were still intact. More recently the V-sign has been associated with Winston Churchill, who used it during the second world war to underline his confident belief that Britain would be victorious. The essential point to bear in mind is that if the first and middle fingers are extended from the fist, and the palm faces back towards the gesturer, it is an insult meaning 'fuck off'.

Italian immigrants tend to have special problems with hand signals because they are used to extravagant displays of gesticulation. They should remember that the British position their hands and fingers differently, and move their arms through different trajectories. The main purpose is to help them formulate what they are saying.

You will have gathered from these brief comments that your right to free speech should not be abused. The French novelist Andre Maurois told a young compatriot who was about to visit Britain: "do not talk too much until you have found your depth. In France it is rude to let a conversation drop; in England it is rash to keep it up. No one there will blame you for silence. When you have not opened your mouth for three years they will think this Frenchman is quite a nice fellow".

It was good advice.

Bloody Foreigners

The good news is that you can be as rude as you like about the French, Germans, and Italians. This may be a bit hard, at first, if you were one of them before becoming a British citizen but you can get the hang of it by listening to conversations in pubs, reading the *Daily Mail* and watching films about the second world war. Here is a brief guide:

France is our traditional enemy. Don't be misled by attempts to disguise the fact, such as the Entente Cordiale (which we have never bothered to translate into English). We wax lyrical about French food, the climate, and the countryside but have little good to say about the French themselves. They don't think much of us either. The British, they claim, are arrogant, lacking in sex appeal, and poor cooks.

This long-standing animosity has not deterred British people from settling in France. Many see it as a way of regaining territory that has always belonged to us without the tiresome business of fighting another war. They have brought in everything to avoid having to eat frog's legs and snails. They say "excuse my French" when using expletives but few actually speak the language and they certainly don't seek to acquire French citizenship. (Imagine having to sing the bellicose national anthem).

There are more than 200,000 French residents in Britain but they are just as determined to maintain their own identity. We don't mind as long as they stick to making sauces.

Germany is a more recent enemy, and we have yet to come to terms with the fact that they are now supposed to be allies. We seldom, if ever, go on holiday there and have no territorial ambitions. We used to mock their passion for hard work but, these days, prefer to draw attention to their pathetic efforts to match Britain's economic performance.

The Germans have bought many of our companies (best not to mention that) but they should not expect to be treated as equals or to assume that we understand their language – one of the main sources of British humour. German immigrants should *always* apologise for the war and make it clear that they hated the Austrian monster, Adolf Hitler. It is, however, permissible to point out that Germany makes good cars.

Italy also fought against us, but we have forgiven the Italians because they never did us any serious harm and because we found their strutting little *Duce* quite hilarious. They have also made up for it since by opening restaurants, cafes, and ice cream parlours all over Britain. They are more popular than other Europeans because they know their place – they don't claim to be superior to the British and, unlike the French, don't presume to lecture us. We like their music and appreciate the attempts made by Luciano Pavarotti to sing in English. They also make nice suits and handbags.

Many of us have holiday homes in Tuscany – known to the British as Chiantishire. We don't bring our own food because we are fond of pasta and no-one forces us to eat frog's legs and snails.

Poland and other countries in Eastern Europe had such a hard time under communist rule that we feel sorry for them. Most immigrants have no idea whatsoever about British culture, but we are willing to teach them provided they recognise that they must earn the privileges attached to citizenship by performing menial tasks such as cleaning, fruit-picking, and digging up roads. It is bad form to jump the queue for council houses or hospital appointments.

Commonwealth Countries are a problem the British have yet to solve. We like Australians and Canadians, who are not regarded as foreigners but as 'kith and kin' – even though many are not from the motherland. We have, however, made it more difficult for them to settle in Britain because the bureaucrats in Brussels take a different view. Complaints should be addressed to the European Commission. Jokes about Australians and Canadians are permitted provided they are not made by Indians, Pakistanis, the French, the Germans, or the Italians.

Other Commonwealth countries are a separate issue. Everyone knows the reason but it should not be mentioned in public – you risk prosecution if you do so. Don't assume that you can get away with it if you come from India or Pakistan; past differences no longer matter now that you are British, and you should not make disparaging remarks about other immigrants unless they are French, German or Italian.

The Chinese are seldom criticised because they keep a low profile and make excellent spring rolls. We still have our doubts about the Japanese but they, too, seldom make a fuss and we love their sushi.

We don't much care what other Europeans think of us. The British may be embarrassed by the behaviour of our football hooligans, and some-times feel the need to disown them, but the media shows little interest in the opinions of our neighbours. This is partly because most journalists cannot be bothered to learn another language (and therefore cannot read foreign newspapers) but it also reflects a tendency to regard their observations as irrelevant, particularly if they are critical. When, occasionally, the press reports some adverse comment it is invariably called an 'outrage'.

Snakes and Ladders

You may, at some stage, want to go into politics. This is one of the privileges you acquired when you became a citizen. Your motive would, no doubt, be entirely honourable – to protect the rights of others like you and help introduce new laws that will make Britain a better country. (No-one does it for the money. The pay is far from generous and you won't be allowed to accept envelopes stuffed with cash – a common practice in some other parts of the world).

By all means have a go at becoming a member of Parliament – the Westminster version – but before doing so you need to know what you will be letting yourself in for.

The first requirement is to decide which party you feel most comfortable with. Keep in mind that, if you make the wrong choice, you may have to spend years in opposition, in which case your opportunity to change anything will be slim. The next and far from being easy step is to get adopted by a constituency. There is bound to be stiff competition, even for a hopeless seat, and you will be closely questioned about everything, including your private life and your views on hanging.

If you manage to get past that daunting hurdle, you will come face to face with a wider audience at an Election – the voters. This involves strolling around the local high street, accosting strangers who generally feel that they have more important things to do than to listen to your spiel, and knocking on as many doors as possible. You may have eggs thrown at you (a venerable British tradition) and must expect many doors to be slammed in your face by people who don't like the look of you or who detest the leader of your party because they have seen too much of him, or her, on television.

Still keen? Very well, let us assume that you win and can now add the letters 'MP' to your name. You will quickly discover, if you have not already done so, that there is no job description for a member of parliament and that you will have little say in what really matters, even if your party is in government. You are required to vote for whatever the leadership has in mind, which may or may not be consistent with the promises made to electorate. Rebels are sharply rebuked by the 'whips' – a term derived from the 'whippers-in' who control packs of hounds.

If you behave there is a chance that you will eventually become a junior minister. The title 'minister' may seem impressive, but you still won't be able to *do* much and there is an ever-present risk that your Leader will replace you in the next 'reshuffle' – often compared to the old board game of snakes and ladders. If the media decides to embark on a witch-hunt, perhaps because you have had too many off-duty dinners with your secretary, you are unlikely to survive even if you have done your best to please him. (Some ministers jump before they are pushed: the usual form is to announce that you want to spend more time with your family).

Many MP's insist that they are not ambitious – their commitment to constituency work, they say, is the heart of what they came into politics for. This may be humbug, a convenient excuse for not getting one's foot on the ladder, but looking after constituents is certainly important. The demands are incessant and call for the stamina of a long-distance runner and the patience of a saint. You will be expected to open garden fetes, speak at Rotary Club dinners and meetings of the Women's Institute, make small talk at wine-and-cheese evenings, attend fund raising events, answer letters from constituents who object to your party's line on immigration and pensions, and hold weekend 'surgeries' for people who think you have an obligation to fix the leaking roof of their council house. The Prime Minister and other members of the Cabinet may be able to get away with excuses ("I have to go to a meeting with the President of the United States") but the run-of-the-mill MP is not granted the same privilege.

What most members of parliament find truly upsetting is the voters tend to be so *ungrateful* – you slog away, week after week, and the buggers are liable to turf you out at the next election because they think that someone else is more likely to fix that damned roof.

If you genuinely wish to have a say in Britain's future you should seek to become a senior civil servant, editor of a national newspaper, presenter of the *Today* programme on radio, or a 'political adviser'. It will spare you the tiresome and unpredictable business of getting elected and you will be viewed as a major player. You could well end up in the House of Lords, where you will be free to express your own opinions without having to worry that you will get the sack – membership is for life.

Alternatively, you may wish to have your say in the Scottish Parliament, Welsh Assembly, or one of England's many council chambers. It will give you status in your local community and, unlike most of the Westminster players, you won't have the expense of maintaining two homes.

You also have the option of standing as an independent candidate or even launching your own party. Many people have done so, often with a bizzare agenda. We have had the Anti Pavement Fouling League, the Teddy Bear Alliance, the Fancy Dress Party, and all sorts of other idiotic attempts to gain attention. One character, who called himself Screaming Lord Sutch, achieved national fame as founder of the Monster Raving Looney Party. He stood in nearly forty elections of one kind or another, advocating policies such as putting crocodiles in the River Thames and banning January and February to make winter shorter. He eventually hanged himself with a multi-coloured skipping rope, presumably because he felt it was a fitting end for a Leader.

The 'European Conspiracy'

There is another option: you could try to secure one of the 732 seats in the European parliament. It's a cushy job because you wouldn't have to do anything.

Some of the Brits who are already MEP's feel that their primary task is to prevent foreigners from making new laws. But if that seems like too much effort you could simply turn up and collect your pay.

The only problem is that the people whose votes you need are liable to ask for your views on 'Europe'. The safest course is to remain silent, but you may *have* to express an opinion. Be warned: even a hint that the European Union is not such a bad idea, all things considered, is bound to be met with hostility.

We British, you see, have quarrelled about this for decades and many of us have taken up entrenched positions. There are Europhiles (for), Europhobes (against) and Eurosceptics who are prepared to concede that there may be a case for 'staying in' but who object to 'giving up our sovereignty and national identity'.

Harold MacMillan, a former prime minister, sought to deal with the issue many years ago. He said that "practically every nation, including our own, has already been forced by the pressures of the modern world to abandon large areas of sovereignty and to realise that we are all inter-dependant". Later Tory governments signed the Single European Act and the Maastricht Treaty, which created European citizenship, and parliament gave its approval after a prolonged and often chaotic debate. John Major said that "I want us to be where we belong. At the very heart of Europe. Working with our partners to build the future".

This should have settled the matter, but he was followed by two Tory leaders with a different approach. William Hague came up with a new slogan: 'In Europe, but not run by Europe'. His campaign at the next general election was largely based on a pledge to 'save the pound'. He told voters: "If you believe in an independent Britain, then come with me and I will give you back your country". It was a bad miscalculation: the Tories lost and he decided to resign. The party, alas, failed to heed the obvious lesson. It replaced him with a Europhobe, Ian Duncan Smith. He, in turn, was forced to make way for the Eurosceptic Michael Howard, whose line is to vote 'no' in the promised referendum on a new European constitution and then to seek 'renegotiation'.

You may well find all this confusing. Why do the Tories keep changing their tune? The short answer is that many Brits, particularly the English, still think that the EU is a fiendish conspiracy by old enemies – France and Germany – to set up a European superstate controlled by them. Napoleon and Hitler tried to do it but came to a sticky end: we fought them and, by God, we will do so again.

There is a strong element of nostalgia in the politics of the Europhobes. They cannot forget that Britain once ruled a mighty Empire and are unwilling to come to terms with the realities of the 21st century. A veritable alphabet soup of anti-EU groups have emerged and withered over the years, reminiscent of the People's Front of Judea in *Monty Python's Life of Brian* – not least because the only people they hate more than European federalists are each other.

The most prominent recent addition is the United Kingdom Independence Party, which advocates withdrawal from the European Union. The cover of its manifesto depicts three nappy-clad babies, adding: "This is their country – make sure it stays that way". Inside it proclaims five essential rights for voters, including freedom from Brussels, freedom from crime, and freedom from 'overcrowding'. Britain, it claims, 'is already full up. We are bursting at the seams'. The message is plain: no more immigration.

The Tories have dismissed the UKIP party as a bunch of 'cranks and political gadflies'. Newspaper columnists have come up with other labels, such as 'BNP in Blazers' and 'the political wing of the Rotary Club'. Its membership certainly includes some strange people. One of the party's most strident supporters is Joan Collins, an elderly actress who says that she is "violently against the European constitution, which will irrevocably bind us to many countries we have been in conflict with for centuries". Ms Collins is "proud to be English", but that hasn't prevented her from spending most of her life in America and in the South of France. Asked how she had voted before her attachment to the UKIP, she said without shame that she had not voted before because she was "never in England at voting time".

Chris Patten, a former EU Commissioner and now Chancellor of Oxford University, says that the party's members "live in a fantasy world of conspiracies against gallant Blighty, white cliffs, Dambusters, Panzer helmets, a world in which every foreigner is a threat, which is totally at variance with the one in which we have to earn our living and keep the peace". Robert Kilroy-Silk, who quit the UKIP after it rejected his bid for the leadership, says that some of the members are "bloody right-wing fascist nutters".

The party has no chance of winning a general election, (it fared badly in the last one) but the Tories (who also lost) worry that it may take votes away from them in the future. It explains their line: what people want, they believe, is Euroscepticism with attitude.

But hang on, we have a *Labour* government. The current prime minister, Tony Blair, is a Europhile (sort of) who has already signed the new constitution and who is confident that *his* party will remain in power. The referendum, he says, will be "a battle between reality and myth". The reality, according to him, is that withdrawal from the EU would have serious consequences for British business and jobs. The myth is that the French and Germans are engaged in a conspiracy. Voters have been fooled into genuinely thinking that the EU will give us straight bananas, compulsory driving on the right, and the replacement of the Queen as head of state. It's all hokum. There will be 'red lines' which define areas where Britain will not concede control – taxation, defence, criminal justice, and the liberty to strike.

It is well nigh impossible to convey the case for the constitution with reverting to the most simplistic 'in or out' argument. The 'out' battle will be fought with slogans and crude soundbites. No-one can predict the outcome with any degree of certainty, but it may turn out to be academic anyway because the Treaty has to be approved by all the 25 member countries, some of which may say 'no'.

I am a Europhile, but some of my friends are Europhobes. Others agree with both sides, which you may feel is a typically British compromise. There is a third course: you can just ignore the whole business. This, opinion polls have shown, is what many people intend to do because they find it too complex, nasty, and *boring*. The young, especially can't see what the fuss is about. They have been to 'Europe' and like it; they have forged new friendships and got used to handling the euro. For many of them, one of the main attractions of the EU is that it offers a wider choice of where to live and work. They didn't fight in the second world war and, like other young Europeans, have no interest in starting another – except in the European football championships.

The Special Relationship

Here is another oddity: many of the Brits who so vehemently oppose the European constitution express great admiration for America – a federal union on a continental scale. They talk fondly of our 'special relationship' and argue that we should build on *that* instead of joining in attempts to create a United States of Europe.

What makes their passionate attachment to the idea even more puzzling is that America is a nation largely built by immigrants and, today, the kind of multi-ethnic, multi-racial society which they don't want to see in Britain.

When and how did this 'special relationship' come about and is it reality or myth?

Historians point out that America was a very British creation. The first settlers came from these isles and brought with them a distinct culture including the English language, Protestant values, individualism, religious commitment, and respect for the law. Then in the eighteenth century they had to define America ideologically to justify their independence from the motherland. We all know what happened: Britain lost her colony. The South later decided to withdraw from the Union and there was a bloody civil war. In the century that followed, Britain and America fought and defeated a common foe: Germany.

The historical background is important because it helps to explain why so many of us still regard the United States as our best friend. The British government was a staunch ally in its war against Iraq, despite the reservations of our European neighbours. We bestow honorary knighthoods on distinguished Americans, offer 'wise counsel', and tell them how much we love their country.

What many Brits choose to forget, or ignore, is that later waves of immigrants changed America. The twentieth century saw a massive influx of other Europeans – Italians, Germans, Scandinavians, Irish, Poles. The American 'melting pot' also absorbed many Chinese and Hispanic immigrants. The US now has a foreign-born population of 26 million, nearly one tenth of its residents. A large percentage is of Hispanic origin and in many parts of the country it is now essential to be bilingual. The 'new' Americans have never heard of the 'special relationship' and even those who have tend to dismiss it as an outdated and irrelevant slogan. As they see it, Britain is just as small European nation which should settle for the role of obedient poodle. Oh, yeah, they loved the Beatles and thought that Princess Diana was cute. Rod Stewart and Elton John are cool, James Bond is almost as tough as Tom Cruise, and that English guy with the rubber face, Mr Bean, is kind of funny. But hey, man, who cares about *history?*

The British public thinks it knows America because we have seen so much of it in movies and on TV. America is Hollywood, New York, Las Vegas, and Disneyworld. We are familiar with the White House because our prime minister goes there so often to meet the President. (The White House, incidentally, is said to have got its name because the exterior was covered with heavy white paint after British troops set fire to the place in 1814. Best not mention that to the Americans).

Many white, protestant Brits who cross the Atlantic for the first time are dismayed to find that they are treated as *foreigners*. It isn't at all what they had expected. British muslims and blacks are less naive: they know that they will encounter prejudice.

The reality is that the special relationship has always been one-sided. In 1982, the State Department declined to support Britain over the Falklands until President Reagan intervened, and successive US governments turned a blind eye to IRA fund-raising. American foreign policy consists entirely of self-interest. We should not delude ourselves that the US will do us any special favours.

The President claims to be 'leader of the free world', but we have no say in who gets elected to the job – or, for that matter, in the choice of senators, congressmen, judges, and dog-catchers. Closer links with the US would not change that simple fact. We British should ask ourselves if we really want to be locked into an American bear hug instead of playing a key role in Europe.

There is, of course, no reason why we should not establish and nurture close *personal* relationships. I have many American friends and a modest apartment in Florida. We may disagree about all sorts of political issues but get on well in everyday life. Having a common language (more or less) undoubtedly helps.

Generalisations can be misleading, but there are some things that make us different. Americans tend to be more direct and intense. They consider their first duty and obligation is to look after Number One. They think that new is good, admire money more openly, don't hesitate to complain, and readily discard something – or someone – that doesn't work. There is little sympathy for people who blame 'bad luck'. They don't eat hamburgers with a knife and fork, even if they are huge and sloppy. They call pudding 'dessert', and don't understand what we have against ice cubes. They are more patriotic (a prime example of the American adage is that anything worth doing is worth overdoing) and more religious provided that everyone accepts that God is a Christian. They can't understand why Brits are addicted to a boring game like cricket, and insist on calling football 'soccer', even though their own version of the world's most popular sport involves running around with the ball in their hands. They think that they invented golf, which the Scots find particularly annoying because they thought of it first. Some are under the impression that we all live in castles and are surprised to find, when they visit us, that we don't throw chicken bones over our shoulder at dinner, like the king who axed all those wives, and that some hotels have air-conditioning and modern furniture. We forgive them, not only because we regard ourselves as an exceptionally tolerant society but also because Americans still pay us the compliment of calling our country Great Britain.

A Place in The Sun

You may find it puzzling that so many of your fellow citizens prefer to live abroad – quite possibly in the country you have come from. Why should they want to leave? More than a million have done so in the last ten years and their number is expected to grow to four million by 2020.

Researchers have made detailed studies of this extraordinary development and have come up with several explanations. The most obvious is that they are fed up with the British weather. It may appeal to tourists from parts of the world where the sun shines every day, and the summers are unbearably hot, but few of us enjoy the grey skies and rain which Britain has in such abundance. A less obvious reason is that they – the deserters – are 'disillusioned', a vague term that embraces everything from traffic jams and the state of our railways to the widespread belief that Britain is being 'swamped' by immigrants.

Some also see it as a good way to avoid the growing tax burden imposed by Chancellors of the Exchequer who regard the 'redistribution of wealth' as their primary mission. They are dismayed when they discover, too late, that other European countries are just as eager to pick their pockets. The only way to dodge income tax is to head for an overcrowded haven like Monaco or one of the palm-fringed islands of The Bahamas, where the cost of living tends to be so high that the benefits turn out to be illusory and where you may die, sooner than expected, from a disease not acknowledged by the medical profession – boredom.

At one time only the rich could afford to buy a home abroad. Today people from all walks of life talk enthusiastically about their 'place in the sun'. Taxi drivers, plumbers, carpenters and other 'working-class' people who used to go on holiday in Blackpool or Clacton are particularly fond of Spain. So many Brits have homes there that in some parts of the Costa del Sol, English is the main language (which saves them the trouble of having to learn Spanish). Best bitter is on tap, HP sauce and Heinz baked beans can be bought in British-owned shops, and you are more likely to find fish and chips on the menu than paella.

'Middle -class' Brits tend to prefer France or Italy. They are entranced by the sight of crumbling ruins, which they are determined to 'do up'. Some want to use them as holiday homes but many are more ambitious. They have romantic visions of a new life as the proprietor of a guest house, olive farm, or thriving vineyard. They give up well-paid jobs, sell their houses in Wimbledon or Birmingham, and embark on what they are confident will be a rewarding venture. They often forget to ask about local taxes and regulations, and they are surprised to discover that it often rains in winter, that customers can be elusive, that they will have to work hard, and that not everyone in their chosen community welcomes their presence. (In parts of rural France expats have awoken to find graffiti slogans like 'Brits out' sprayed on their car bonnets or the walls of their home – the kind of thing that they know happens to immigrants who have come over to Britain but which they never expected to be done to them).

Most of us take it for granted that we can settle anywhere we want, at any time we want. This is certainly true of other nations in the European Union, but it is much more difficult in the case of countries like the United States, Canada and Australia. They have their own economic problems and immigration is tightly controlled. White migrants still have a better chance than blacks or Asians, but they face barriers in many places where they were once the dominant force, such as South Africa and the Caribbean islands. This isn't surprising: they, too, want to protect the economic interests of their citizens and don't like to be reminded that they used to be part of the British colonies.

Ironically, the most 'patriotic' Brits can often be found abroad. They may no longer wish to live in the land of their birth but they have strong views on what kind of country Britain ought to be (which generally turns out to be based on nostalgic recollections of the imperial past) and cling tenaciously to what they consider to be British modes of dress and to traditional customs like afternoon tea with cucumber sandwiches, parties on the Queen's birthday, cricket matches, and flying the Union Jack on a flagpole in their English gardens. They disapprove of what is happening 'back home', and have no desire to return, but feel entitled to have their say about the way we are governed and to complain about the 'invasion' of Britain by foreigners who have given up their place in the sun.

The Country

It is, of course, perfectly feasible to change one's lifestyle without leaving Britain. Many of us prefer to 'escape to the country'.

Foreigners tend to be puzzled by the expression, so let me make it clear what it means. We are not talking about 'this country' or 'our country', but the countryside. It can be anything from a tranquil village to a small market town. There are no borders, so it is often hard to tell where suburbia ends and 'the country' begins. Look out for grazing cows, ducks paddling serenely on ponds, thatched cottages, pubs with silly names, landrovers hogging narrow lanes, and teenagers on horses.

What you need to know is that the countryside is predominately white. It is the heartland of English conservatism and racial prejudice is rampant. You are more likely to be accepted if your skin is the same colour but even that cannot be taken for granted. Many country folk object to the 'invasion' of their area by affluent middle-class whites from London and other cities. One of the main complaints is that they have pushed up house prices to such an extent that local first-time buyers don't stand a chance of finding a place they can afford. (But ask a countryman if he is willing to sell his own property to a deserving native for a lower sum and the answer will be 'no'.) Another charge is that they are making little contribution because they only come for weekends and holidays. The townies say this is unfair because they create jobs – most employ gardeners, housekeepers and builders. They also claim that they are helping to safeguard services like shops and post offices.

Many have become full-time members of the community because they have retired or are working from home.

There is no law against escaping to 'the country' but it is hard to cope with prejudice. You should certainly talk to others who have made the move before you commit yourself. The obvious place for this is the local pub, but try to get an invitation to spend a weekend with one of the 'invaders'.

You will naturally want to know how to fit in. This requires some basic understanding of country life. Don't turn up in clothes that instantly mark you out as a townie and potential intruder – a suit, a pinstripe shirt, tasselled loafers. Buy or borrow a tweed jacket and corduroy trousers. You will also need a pair of Wellington boots, so that you can stroll across muddy fields on Sunday morning. When you go into the pub, order a pint of beer and tell everyone that you adore dogs and horses. Don't bring up the subject of religion: country folk love God but don't want to hear about Allah.

Some people maintain that rural Wales is a better bet. It certainly has some delightful scenery, and you may be able to buy a cottage for a reasonable price, but the Welsh are just as reluctant to welcome outsiders – especially if they are English. It helps if you can sing, are fond of sheep, don't mind the rain, and are prepared to learn their strange language.

Scotland has also attracted 'invaders' from the south. The Scots (note the spelling) are shrewd people who are willing to flog dilapidated property for large sums of money but they don't like the English either. You have a considerable advantage if you were born on the continent, especially in France. Be sure to stress that you enjoy the sound of bagpipes, prefer haggis to fish and chips, and consider Robbie Burns to be a greater poet than William Shakespeare.

The main problem with living in 'the country' is that you are liable to get bored. This is what has happened to many townies who escaped without giving much thought to what they were going to *do* when they got there. Run a farm? Hard work, monotonous, and often unrewarding. Grow your own vegetables? Ditto. Make jam, gossip with the neighbours, feed chickens, prune roses, shoot birds and rabbits? Fun, but for how long? Working from home may also get tedious. Many people who have tried it say they feel isolated: they miss the office and fear neglect.

There is an alternative: you could move to the seaside. This is what most people did before they heard about sunny countries like Spain, and companies like Thomas Cook and Thomson started to sell cheap package holidays. When I was chairman of the English Tourist Board, in the early 1990s, I launched a national campaign with the slogan: 'England's seaside, for the fun of it". I was widely mocked, because it seemed a hopeless cause, but since then we have seen a remarkable change. Seaside towns that used to be shunned have attracted a new generation of escapists, including many immigrants. They have become more cosmopolitan, particularly in Devon and Cornwall. Go there if you can cook, know how to grow palm trees, and think you can earn a living as a painter, sculptor, writer, builder, potter or gardener. You can wear what you want and you don't have to join protest marches organised by the Countryside Alliance. You don't even have to laugh at the mother-in-law jokes told by entertainers who were household names thirty years ago.

Keeping Up With The Kumars

Surveys have shown that 65 per cent of Britons live in Suburbia. Foreigners sometimes complain that it isn't mentioned in their travel guides or that they can't find it on a map. The simple explanation is that there is no such place: Suburbia is what we call residential areas just outside a town or a city.

As with 'the country', it is often difficult to tell where they begin. Many suburbs seem to consist entirely of rows and rows of identical houses, each with its own little patch of green. The main difference is that they tend to have names instead of numbers – an attempt to express individuality that often turns out to be absurdly pretentious. Some also have gnomes or moulded imitations of pink flamingoes in their front garden.

Country folk look down on Suburbia because it 'lacks character'. They are just as critical of the residents. Calling someone 'suburban' is meant as an insult: it implies that he or she is narrow-minded, conformist, plebeian.

Suburbanites say that such snooty generalisations are unfair. They point out that the better areas have homes of all shapes and sizes, tree-lined streets, neat gardens, clipped laurel hedges, smart shops, and better restaurants than one is likely to find in 'the country'. Most of the residents are affluent (and interesting) middle-class people who have chosen to live there because they value their privacy and because they want to bring up their children in that kind of environment rather than in a crowded and noisy city.

Dr Vesna Goldworthy, a founder of Britain's first Centre for Suburban Studies, says that the image of our suburbs is stuck in the 1970's. They are, she claims, fast becoming multi-racial, multi-coloured, multi-everything. A jovial Serb, she talks with enthusiasm about 'Korean New Malden' and 'Punjabi Southall'.

Dr Goldsworthy plainly regards this as a welcome trend. What you need to know, if you don't already, is that many Brits disagree. They resent the fact that suburbs like Southall have been taken over by immigrants and their offspring, and have no wish to be part of a multi-racial community. They prefer an area which, to put it bluntly, is more 'white'. You may find this deplorable, but there is no law against it. (Nor, for that matter, is there a law which requires Asians and blacks to live in enclaves. They, too, are entitled to choose. The main barrier tends to be financial: homes in upmarket 'white' suburbs are generally more expensive).

One thing that suburbanites appear to have in common, besides the habit of giving their house a name, is a passion for home improvement. It explains why there are so many DIY stores, garden centres, and television programmes offering professional advice.

You have no doubt come across the expression: 'keeping up with the Joneses'. It means striving to have as nice a home as one's neighbours. If Dr Goldsworthy is right (as she certainly is about suburbs like Southall) we should also be talking about 'keeping up with the Kumars'.

The trouble is that the Joneses and Kumars tend to move the goalposts. Just when you think that you have caught up with them they put in a new bathroom or kitchen, build a conservatory, and make other improvements which you can't afford to match without getting into serious debt.

You may be tempted to drop in, so that you can check up on all this, but it should not be taken for granted that they will be pleased to see you. Suburbanites hate being caught unprepared. Always phone first. They may invite you to come for tea, but there are several rules to bear in mind. Don't demand a guided tour; leave it to them to decide what they want to show you. Don't express a critical opinion; you may think that the new furniture is hideous but they expect compliments, not honesty. And don't boast about your own home improvements; it will only make them even more determined to stay ahead.

You are not, of course, *forced* to keep up. The neighbours will not complain if you don't. They are more likely to be relieved. You will, however, upset them if the exterior of your own house starts to look shabby – an eyesore is liable to affect the market value of nearby property. Give your doors and windows a new coat of paint from time to time, but avoid garish colours. Wash the net curtains at least once a year. Make sure that the front garden is tidy. Don't bother with gnomes and flamingoes; they are considered to be frightfully vulgar. And there is no need to plant a flagpole, and run up the Union Jack, to show how patriotic you are. A National Trust sticker in your window is sufficient proof that you have made an effort to integrate.

Suburbanites have another grand passion: their car. It is as important as a new bathroom or kitchen, if not more so, because everyone can *see* it. A posh car like a Mercedes makes them feel socially superior and is usually parked outside the house, even if they have a garage. The proud owner will polish it every week and will be delighted if the neighbours are envious.

Suburbia, and our perceptions of it, will continue to change. Areas which a few decades ago were said to have a dismal future have become fashionable. Others have declined but could well see renewed prosperity in the years ahead. Immigration is one factor but it isn't the only one. Many more 'natives' may decide that suburbs suit them. They offer easy access to city life, if and when they want it, and an equally good opportunity to make occasional forays into 'the country' without getting involved in the obsessions of the green-wellied whingers.

'Bonking for Britain'

Economists, who are trained to worry about everything, say that Britain faces a crisis unless we have more children. This is because the population is ageing and, before long, there won't be enough young people to sustain the lifestyle of the older generation. Immigrants, they maintain, should be welcomed because they are more productive. Some newspapers have put it more bluntly: if you want to make yourself useful you must 'bonk for Britain'.

What, you may ask, has gone wrong? Have we lost interest in sex? Did the title of a hugely popular West End play, *No Sex, Please, We're British* reflect a fundamental change in attitude?

The short answer is 'no'. The show was meant to be a farce. We have late night porn channels on television and a cornucopia of erotic publications which can be found on the top shelf of most newsagents. The press gives massive coverage to the sexual indiscretions of cabinet ministers, TV presenters, and other public figures. Sales of Viagra are booming. Women's magazines provide explicit advice on how to have better orgasms.

Sex clearly remains a subject of absorbing interest. We talk about it, write and read about it, and make jokes about it. Some of us may be too tired to *do* it, after a hard day at the office, but there is no truth in the rumour – spread by the French – that we have forgotten how to copulate or prefer a life of celibacy.

What is true is that many of us no longer have the urge to *procreate*. As in France and other western countries, birth rates have been falling for some years. They are at their lowest level since records began. It doesn't mean that we have given up sex. The main reason is that so many women no longer see motherhood as their primary function. One in five now reaches the age of 40 without having children, according to official statistics. More than a third of pregnancies in women under 20 ends in abortion.

Some people – mostly men – blame the feminist movement. It has encouraged them to focus on their careers, which they have done with alarming success. 'Having it all' has become an objective that doesn't include taking care of howling infants. It *does* include having sex with a variety of attractive partners.

The birthrate has declined for another reason: a large and growing number of our fellow citizens are 'gay'. This used to mean a cheerful personality but the word has been hijacked by homosexuals and lesbians. Sex between consenting adults over 21 became legal in 1967. Since then there has also been a marked change in attitudes. Gay people used to be so afraid of prosecution, and abuse, that many went to great lengths to hide their sexual desires. Some tried to sublimate them in marriage and a family because they wanted to be able to live a 'normal life'. Being gay was 'the love that dare not speak its name'. Today they live openly with partners, or feel able to acknowledge publicly that they are gay. They can be as flamboyant as they wish, and there are dating agencies and campaigns on 'gay issues'. What many of us still regard as unacceptable, however, is that lesbians should have children or that male partners should be able to adopt them.

A famous British star of the stage, Mrs Patrick Campbell, said that "it doesn't matter what you do in the bedroom as long as you don't do it in the street and frighten the horses". This still applies, but we have become more tolerant. There is certainly no need to be concerned about the horses: they vanished from our streets when Henry Ford invented cheap cars.

Pagan societies encouraged the young to breed through a programme of sexually-charged fertility dances. Our political masters reckon that 'family friendly' policies are likely to be more effective in the 21st century. The Government plans to increase paid maternity leave and to introduce tax breaks for childcare.

Australia has gone one step further: women are being paid $3000 dollars for each baby they have. The Finance Minister has urged couples to have at least three children, including 'one for the country'. Two, he points out, are not enough because "you are not making a net improvement". Local authorities in Italy are also offering cash incentives.

Britain does not, at present, provide such direct bribes. It may do so in future, but many immigrants are quite willing to breed without them. Nearly one in five births are to mothers born outside Britain, mostly in nations such as Pakistan and Bangladesh and countries in the Caribbean. The percentage is higher in Greater London and in cities like Manchester, Bradford and Birmingham. Some of us find this disturbing but they are the next generation of taxpayers. If we are not prepared to 'bonk for Britain' we should not complain if the new citizens do so.

The Parent Trap

If you already have children, or intend to procreate, keep this in mind: *everything that goes wrong with them is your fault.*

You may feel that they are to blame for bad behaviour, or that 'society' is responsible, but that is not how psychologists and other experts see it. If your child goes off the rails it is because you have failed as a parent.

Every country has its own rules and codes, but you need to know what is expected from you in Britain.

Make an early start.

The process of indoctrination must start before the age of 5. If you wait for your child to be old enough for good manners to matter it will probably be too late. (British teenagers make their own rules). Toddlers should not be permitted to throw their food at you, scream whenever they want instant attention, climb on other people's furniture, swear, talk with their mouth full, and fart or pick their noses in the presence of guests.

The snag, of course, is that kids have a nasty habit of doing what they have *seen* you do, not what you told them to do. It is your duty to set a good example.

Teach them respect for authority.

In Victorian times this was usually done by fathers with terrifying beards. If they were too busy, or simply not up to it, the job was delegated to a nanny – a stern, middle-aged spinster who tackled it with brisk, no-nonsense efficiency.

Many experts say that standards have declined mainly because fathers have become too soft and because only the rich can afford to employ a nanny. The middle-classes tend to make do with an *au pair*, but this often turns out to be a mistake because young, undomesticated foreign girls are liable to be on the side of the children. Working class parents usually have to rely on elderly relatives, but they tend to be even more soft-hearted than dads.

What the experts and other critics seldom acknowledge is that parents have been deprived of a tool which, in the past, was the principal means of teaching respect for authority: the cane.

Let me make it quite clear: hitting a child, even if it's your own, can get you into serious trouble with the law.

The issue was recently debated in the House of Lords. Some of their lordships, possibly influenced by painful childhood experiences, wanted to make all smacking a criminal offence, subject to up to five years in jail. Others were reluctant to go that far. A compromise was eventually agreed on. It allows *mild* smacking provided it doesn't cause bruising, scratching, reddening of the skin or mental harm and is not carried out by an implement. Asked to define mild smacking, a Queen's Counsel who specialises in child and human rights law said that it means "a light tap".

OK? Well, probably not. Most children, especially those living in rough neighbourhoods, would laugh at such feeble attempts to impose discipline. A light tap? Tell that to the school bully who thinks that the best way to get respect is to give other kids a bloody nose.

Some parents believe, naively, that teachers will do the job for them. The truth is that, in New Britain, most are so scared of pupils, social workers, childcare experts, lawyers, and (yes) parents, that they don't dare to make a stand. Corporal punishment in schools is illegal.

You will naturally want to know what alternative methods are available to you. These include a ban on watching TV, confining a child to his or her room 'until you have learned to behave', and stopping pocket money. The latter may work best because children are obsessed by money.

Another option is to deprive them of their favourite junk food – a form of punishment strongly recommended by the experts because, they say, child obesity has become a serious problem. It is *your fault* if your kids are fat, but you can redeem yourself by refusing to let them have chocolate, crisps, burgers, cakes, fizzy drinks, chips, and packets of Wotsits. Serving nothing but salads and brussels sprouts should bring them to heel, especially if you also deprive them of the means to go out and buy the junk themselves. Remember, though, that the inevitable rebellion cannot be squashed by resorting to violence.

In America, not long ago, one couple resorted to a different tactic: they went on strike. Fed up with serving their children hand and foot without as much as an occasional thank you, they moved into a tent in the front garden of their home, taking the television with them. The kids returned from school to find their parents sitting outside with signs declaring 'Parents on Strike!' and 'Seeking Compassion and Respect'. The son's first reaction was to ask his mother whether she had lost her mind. The daughter showed more understanding. She stunned her parents by doing her own washing just two days into their protest and said that she felt bad that she drove them to take such drastic measures. "I guess we don't help out as much as we could", she admitted. "I'm going to change. I don't want the to do this again".

Some parents prefer to send their teenagers to boarding school. It doesn't guarantee that they will become model citizens, but at least they will become someone else's problem.

Not everyone, of course, can afford to do this. There are nearly seven million adults in Britain whose grown-up children are still living at home with them. More than a million of these 'children' are pushing 40. A friend of mine, whose 38 year old son has defied all attempts to persuade him to leave, says that it drives him mad but that he doesn't know what to do. He is caught in the parent trap: you want to do the 'right thing', are looking for a way out, but find it hard to resist what is plainly a form of emotional blackmail.

There is an obvious solution. Tell them that, from now on, they will have to take care of you – and wave a tearful goodbye as they get into the car you have bought them for their last birthday and head for new pastures.

Going For An Indian

According to government findings, Britain has the highest rate of obesity in Europe. This is not just because so many of our children have become porkers; more than half of all *adults* are overweight, with one in five classified as obese. Far from setting a good example we have given our kids a perfect excuse.

Yeah, we know that fat is ugly and dangerous. But, hey, it's a free country. We have the *right* to stuff our faces with double cheeseburgers, extra-large pizzas, and super-sized chips. We don't want to be lectured by experts. Why don't they mind their own business?

A House of Commons select committee debated the problem in 2004 and published a report. It claimed that an 'obesity epidemic' is sweeping Britain and that the lectures are justified because it's costing the economy £7 billion a year and the National Health Service £3.5 billion. But the committee didn't blame *us* for this alarming state of affairs. The culprit, it said, was the food industry. Manufacturers were using devious advertising methods to sell their products and supermarkets were encouraging people to eat fatty, sugar processed foods by making them cheap. The only way to stop the epidemic was 'to restrict their activities'.

Oh no, it isn't. A better way is to persuade the couch potatoes to eat more sensibly and to take more exercise, because if they don't they will have a heart attack at 40 or get a horrible disease like cancer. In short, scare the hell out of them.

Some commentators maintain that fat is a class issue. Most of the seriously obese, they say, are poor. They can't afford to eat healthy food. What, not even salads and brussels sprouts?

The notion of plump poverty would have struck earlier generations as strange. A century ago the poor were as lean as fence posts. They didn't have supermarkets, fast-food chains, and welfare benefits. They were more worried about where to get the next meal than about getting fat. This was also true of the generation that lived through the second world war. Nearly everything was rationed and people were grateful if the local butcher slipped them an extra pork chop.

Rationing was still in force when I came to Britain as an immigrant, early in 1949, and few of the poor were obese. Working class families grew their own vegetables on 'allotments', kept chickens and rabbits, and generally stayed in good shape.

It still happens. We don't *have* to eat cheeseburgers, or buy cinema-sized containers of popcorn and fizzy drinks, and we can all afford to go for brisk walks, kick a ball around with the kids, or get on a bike. There is, for that matter, no law against going on a diet.

If you don't want to accept responsibility, try this for size: it's all the fault of *foreigners*. Who introduced cheeseburgers to Britain? The Americans. Who got us hooked on pasta? The Italians. Who told us that we need fattening sauces? The bloody French.

Fast-food chains like MacDonald's have 'outlets' everywhere. There are numerous Indian, Chinese, Italian, Greek, Spanish, Thai and French restaurants. High streets have Chinese takeaways and kebab shops. 'Going for an Indian' at weekends has become part of the British way of life; chicken tikka masala is reported to be more popular than fish and chips.

Before these people arrived most of us took little interest in food: all that counted was having enough of it, not how it tasted. *They* turned us into gluttons.

London is said to be the 'gastronomic capital of the world', a claim that would have been regarded as ludicrous in my younger days and which is entirely based on the profusion of foreign restaurants. Menus feature concoctions like 'terrine of fibrous ham knuckle surrounding a melting sweet heart of foie gras, with an inspired garnish of lightly acidulated pease pudding'.

Chefs have become celebrities, strutting around the room like a prize turkey. Waiters treat 'ordinary' customers with disdain, especially if they have the nerve to ask for a translation of the menu. Food critics write at length about the latest culinary fad or the best place for sushi, couscous, and lobster-filled ravioli on lemon grass.

This obsession with novelty is a metropolitan middle class thing, and I accept that it has little to do with the 'obesity epidemic'. (Nouvelle cuisine, a friend of mine says, is French for small portions). The upper classes don't feel the same need to be trendy. The working classes, too, find it absurdly pretentious. A hundred quid for a meal that leaves you hungry? *Come on*.

The average UK supermarket offers some 30,000 products, including a wide range of fruit and vegetables, so we can hardly complain that we have no choice. There is plenty of information about what food is fattening and what is not. We don't need the Government to play nanny.

Many Asian families cook marvellously inventive meals on a low budget and stay slim and healthy. One of the main reasons is that they know what to do with vegetables – a skill I admire but which, like many other Brits, have not yet managed to acquire. Shameful, I know, but it's so easy to open a can of peas.

Tarts and Fruitcakes

You may not care for traditional British food but as a new citizen you should avoid the kind of criticism we get from foreigners like the French. Be loyal to your country. It is also bad form to accept an invitation to dinner in an English home and make it obvious to your hosts that you are not keen on shepherd's pie, Lancashire hotpot, or Cornish pasties. If you can't stand any of that stuff, tell them *in advance* that you are a vegetarian. (Best not to bring religion into it). Most will gladly substitute a large helping of spinach providing you refrain from lecturing your fellow guests on animal rights or the risks they run by eating meat.

London may be the 'gastronomic capital of the world' but many of us are still fond of the 'plain' food we grew up with. It includes pork pies, Scotch eggs, mushy peas, jellied eels, toad in the hole, a Sunday roast with Yorkshire pudding, bangers and mash, and fish and chips. (There is some dispute about the best way to eat fish and chips. Traditionalists maintain that it should be eaten out of a newspaper held hotly in the hand, in the course of an evening's stroll. Others say this is vulgar: they prefer to sit down and use proper utensils).

You are no doubt familiar with the full British breakfast – an assembly of eggs, sausages, fried bread, bacon, baked beans, and mushrooms or black pudding. Doctors warn that it's even more lethal than cheeseburgers and other junk food, but it remains popular. (In Scotland you may be offered porridge and kippers, a healthier combination).

We also take pride in our marmalades and jams, Dover sole, dressed crab, steak and kidney pie, calves liver and onions, oxtail, oysters, Welsh lamb, mutton, scones, smoked salmon, venison, tarts and fruitcakes, and English cheeses. (Even the French concede that Stilton is sublime).

Tea may not be grown in Britain, but we drink more of it than our continental neighbours and have our own version of what the Japanese call a 'tea ceremony'. You may be asked "shall I be mother?", which should not be taken as an invitation to father a child: it means that your host regards it as a sacred duty to fill your cup. You may also be offered cucumber or watercress sandwiches. (The sandwich is, of course, a British invention).

This brings me to another important aspect: table manners. Foreigners may get away with incorrect behaviour because we recognise that they have different customs, but British citizens are expected to know the rules. Unfortunately, this isn't always the case – many people seem to think they don't matter.

An all too common habit, even among adults, is to eat with one's mouth open. It happens because some of us are greedy, or in a hurry, or determined to talk at the same time. The sight of food being masticated is repulsive. The correct procedure is to take small mouthfulls and keep your trap shut until each morsel is safely on the way to the stomach. Not easy if you love to talk – as I do – but essential if one wants to make a favourable impression. You should also avoid the Japanese custom of noisily eating your soup and belching.

Another bad habit is to grab whatever is on the table. It is tempting to do so, especially if your host as been stingy, but you will annoy the other guests. If you want something, first offer it to someone else. He or she should say "after you". Having both been polite, who has the first go is unimportant: you have made the right move.

You should also wait to eat until everyone else has been served. If you don't like the food, (even the spinach) have just a little and explain that you are on a strict diet. You can always raid the fridge when you get home.

If you have enjoyed the meal, don't lick your fingers. It may be OK in Mcdonald's but not at dinner parties. Your host should have provided finger bowls of cold water and a slice of lemon. This should not be confused with soup: dip your fingers in it and dry them with a napkin.

Eating peas can be difficult and should be practised. Spear two or three peas with your fork and hold them in place with your knife: do not shovel them down with a spoon. You *may* squash them first, but be aware that it will identify you as a member of the working class. This also applies to the American custom of drinking from a bottle or can, which sadly has been adopted by many young people.

Flirting at the table is acceptable. Snogging, groping, talking dirty and removing items of clothing is not.

In some middle-class homes, women are still expected to 'withdraw' at the end of the meal so that they can talk about fashion, leaving the men to settle the problems of the world. The women's lib movement has made a largely successful effort to put a stop to that.

If you are eating in a restaurant, remember that it's un-British to summon a waiter by snapping your fingers or bellowing across the room. It may work in countries like Italy and Spain but it is not acceptable in Britain. We prefer to make eye-contact, smile, and indicate that we are ready to order by lifting our eyebrows or nodding. If you have been waiting to get your bill for over 30 minutes, stand up and put your coat on. The waiter will be over in a flash.

British cooking is being reworked by many chefs. There are, however, few upmarket restaurants which specialise in our native cuisine, even in London. Fortunately, most of the food I have listed is available in Sainsbury's and other supermarkets. You can buy some tasty steak and kidney pie and invite your friends round for 'an English'.

You and The Law

Many immigrants are confused by our legal system. This is not surprising: British born citizens often have the same problem. Some blame foreigners, particularly meddling bureaucrats in Brussels, but our own politicians are also alarmingly fond of new rules and regulations. It suits lawyers because they can charge exorbitant fees for interpreting them.

The newspapers now and then give us a glimpse of a High Court Judge in full battle dress – an awesome sight – and the more sensational trials are covered at length because it boosts circulation. But the vast majority of cases attract little attention.

Hardened criminals have the advantage of knowing their rights and what they may be able to get away with. For most of us, however, contact with the law tends to be confined to chats with bored policemen when we have been burgled and occasional visits to a solicitors office to discuss nothing more sinister than a mortgage deed, will, or business contract.

This, alas, is changing. There is a growing risk that you will, at some point, be accused of committing an offence you may not have recognised as such. Here are some helpful guidelines.

Always insist that you are innocent.

The police must *prove* that you have transgressed and will naturally seek to get a confession out of you. (Don't worry: third-degree methods are not permitted in Britain). Insist that you are innocent; if you are not, remember you have the right to remain silent.

The 'verbal confessions' that, from time to time, appear so conveniently in an officer's evidence are often the result of careless talk. "It's a straight cop, guv" or "how do you know it was us that done the job?" before the officer has had a chance to caution the subject, or before he has made his written statement, makes it difficult to conduct a successful defence.

Motorists (who can be forgiven for sometimes thinking that they are Public Enemy No 1) may be tempted to argue, make a joke, offer a bribe, or boast about their 'contacts' when they are stopped by the police. This invariably turns out to be a bad mistake.

Making an officer angry is a sure way of ending up in court. Don't assume that he has a sense of humour or that he will be impressed if you mention that your best friend is a lawyer. Waving a banknote under his nose is a serious offence. Stay calm and say nothing that will make the situation worse.

Don't walk in public parks at 3 am.

This may seem a harmless pastime but your purpose may be misunderstood, especially if you are a politician or an actor. If you feel in desperate need of fresh air be sure to take a dog with you.

Don't fight with your neighbours.

The Law Reports abound with tales of the most unseemly battles between people living next door to each other. Noise, smell, vibrations, animals, fences, trees, plants – all have led to bitter disputes in court. In one case, a man could not stand the noise when the music teacher next door gave his pupils piano lessons. So he took to banging on trays, whistling, and shrieking whenever lessons were given. Result: he was ordered to stop and pay damages.

Always try to find a compromise, even if you *hate* your neighbour. It may be tough, but you won't have to remortgage your home to pay a lawyer's bill.

Don't beat your spouse.

Punishing one's partner for some transgression, real or imagined, may be acceptable in some countries, but in Britain the law will not tolerate domestic violence of any sort. Don't imagine that you will be allowed to get away with it because your partner has an affair with the neighbour or lodger: we are not as passionate or forgiving as the French or the Italians.

This also goes for children who, you may feel, have defied parental authority to an intolerable degree, and to your pets. (The Royal Society for the Prevention of Cruelty to Animals – notice that 'royal' dates from 1824. The protection of children was not made official until 1884).

You may feel safe if you stick to verbal abuse, but even that can't be taken for granted. An aggrieved partner may seek, and get, a divorce and a crippling financial settlement, on the grounds of 'unreasonable behaviour' (this is a civil matter but don't be misled by the adjective: such cases are rarely 'civil').

Don't shoot burglars.

The law allows you to use 'reasonable force' against intruders. This means that if you find a burglar in your kitchen or bedroom at 2 am you will have to decide what a court would consider to be fair. A key factor is whether you are acting in self defence. If you feel threatened you could hit him with a cricket bat, poker, or rolling pin. You could also throw vases, saucepans, lamps, and the TV remote control. If none of these items are in easy reach you may bite his ear off. But you could get into serious trouble if you shoot him. Britain isn't Texas.

The police are very strict about how you keep a gun. You can't hide it under your bed; you have to secure it in a locked cupboard with the key in a secret place. The main reason is to make it difficult for a burglar to steal it. This makes it more or less impossible to get it out, load it, and blast away at the intruder. If you ignore the rules, and kill him, you may be arrested and charged with using 'disproportionate force'.

The standard police advice is that, if you hear someone kicking in the front door, you should escape to a locked room and call 999. It makes sense, but there is no guarantee that help will arrive quickly. You may have read about a homeowner, Tony Gladstone, who was staring out of his window one evening when he saw two youths breaking into his garden shed. He called the police but was told, sorry, there was no patrol available. So he rang back a moment later and said: "Don't hurry, I've just shot them". Within minutes his house was bathed in blue light: there were half a dozen patrol cars on the scene. The senior officer in charge was furious when he discovered that Mr Gladstone had lied.

The Government insists that the law is on the side of the victim, not the offender, but there are limits. You certainly cannot use a gun *outside* your home. Not long ago, a teacher who fired a pellet gun at the feet of a teenage criminal after acts of vandalism against her family was found guilty of 'affray and possessing a firearm with intent to cause fear of violence'. The judge told her: "There can be no excuse whatsoever for what you did. The courts discourage vigilante action and the public are very concerned about the use of firearms in public places". He sent her to jail for six months and said that she would have received a longer sentence were it not for her good character. The Court of Appeal later set this aside and granted her a conditional discharge, but it refused her permission to challenge her convictions for affray and possessing a firearm with intent to cause fear and violence.

Never sue anyone for libel.

As many egocentric people have discovered, suing another British citizen for libel is an expensive, embarrassing, and often futile undertaking. Lawyers can put up a dozen different interpretations on a single word, and you will be dismayed by the length and cost of a trial. You may be outraged by comments someone has made about you in public, but unless you can prove that they were 'racist' or have done irreplaceable harm to your reputation, it is best to 'grin and bear it'. Politicians, authors, and playwrights do it all the time. The offensive remarks will soon be forgotten if you don't make a Big Issue out of them.

Libel is not a crime but telling a lie under oath most certainly is, regardless of which side you are on. Don't even think about it.

If someone sues *you* for libel, it generally makes sense to offer an apology (even if you believe that your remarks were entirely justified) and to persuade your lawyer to settle the matter quietly – difficult but not impossible. You may have to pay damages, but the amount involved is likely to be much smaller than the cost of a courtroom battle.

Look smart.

The police, and British courts, tend to be influenced by the way you look. A good appearance is like a letter of recommendation. There is no actual law about what you should wear in court, but 'proper attire' will make a favourable impression. Jeans, sweaters, bomber jackets, and mops of unruly hair will have the opposite effect.

A fashion designer, summoned for motoring offences, turned up in a suburban court wearing a black and orange cloak, an orange jacket with a frilly off-white lace shirt, trousers, one leg of which was black and the other orange, and carrying an antique gold-topped cane. "Do you regard this as suitable dress to appear in a court of law?" asked the horrified clerk of the court. The designer replied: "It is my usual mode of dress and I hope it will become the thing for the modern gent". The magistrates were not amused: they told him to come back on another day in clothes 'like we wear'.

Women should leave their short skirts at home and refrain from trying to sway the court with a shameless display of shapely legs and ample bosom. Female magistrates find it offensive and will press for severe punishment; their male colleagues on the bench are liable to have a heart attack.

Guilty or not guilty?

You may, at some point, be required to serve on a jury. Some people welcome the opportunity to sit in judgement of a fellow-citizen; others regard it as a daunting and unpleasant task. Whatever your personal views you cannot escape jury service unless you come within one of the exempt categories. These include peers, MP's, practising barristers, prison governors and certified lunatics but *not* shopkeepers, bank managers, corporate whiz-kids, pop stars, models, TV presenters, hairdressers, authors, chefs, waiters, musicians, journalists and others who are reckoned to have the necessary qualifications to decide whether the accused is guilty or not guilty.

It is important to understand, and accept, that juries play a significant role in the administration of British Justice. Our judges seldom fail to pay tribute, in their public utterances, to the splendours of the system, the glories of its history, and the innate sense of fairness of the average British juror. (Their private opinions are something else).

You are, therefore, expected to say you will gladly serve, even if it means having to close your shop for a while or cancelling a planned holiday. The rules are simple. Don't fall asleep in the jury box, talk on your mobile, interrupt the judge, accept a bribe, applaud the speeches made by counsel, wave or wink at the accused or a witness, or smoke. Oh, and don't forget that you should only vote 'guilty' if you have no reasonable doubt. Piece of cake.

Big Brother

The proliferation of laws and regulations has been accompanied by another development you should bear in mind: *everyone is being watched.*

Way back in 1949 the British novelist George Orwell (real name Blair) published a satirical book which portrayed a society – supposedly Britain in 1984 – very much like Stalin's Soviet Union. It was ruled by Big Brother, a tyrant who suppressed all dissent, invented preposterous slogans (War is Peace, Ignorance is Strength) and created a terrifyingly efficient surveillance system. People were constantly reminded that Big Brother is Watching You.

Orwell's grim scenario attracted a lot of publicity at the time but we were confident that nothing like this could happen in a country which had seen off Hitler. It didn't: 1984 came and went without any sign of a dictator. Some people will tell you that Margaret Thatcher came close, but the charge is absurd. She had to justify her decisions in parliament and stand for re-election; she was eventually deposed by her own party.

Journalists like Simon Heffer of the *Daily Mail*, that self-appointed champion of the middle classes, would have you believe that the Labour Government has turned our country into a police state.

"It is", he maintains, "almost as if Britain is being Sovietised, with a central committee that decides what we can do and, to an increasingly alarming extent, think." This, too, is nonsense. If it were true, Heffer would be in jail. Police states don't allow criticism.

I have always taken the view that zealous bureaucrats are the real threat. They are the people we have to deal with on a regular basis and many are arrogant busybodies, eager to interfere as much as possible in our lives. It's the Little Brothers (and Sisters) who are most likely to give us a hard time. They get away with it because, unlike politicians, they are seldom named and shamed in the media.

Orwell was right about one thing: we have all become subject to surveillance in one form or another. More than four million CCTV cameras have been installed in recent years. They are everywhere – on roads and motorways, and in airports, railway stations, schools, hospitals, libraries, sports venues, car parks and other public places. The official line is that they help to prevent crime and make it easier to convict thieves and muggers who have been caught on tape. It seems so logical that there has been barley a squeak of public protest, but many of us worry about possible abuse. We don't like the idea of being spied on by an all-seeing eye.

What you need to know is that if you join a rally or march you may be photographed or filmed and put on a list of terrorist suspects. This is not an Orwellian fantasy: it has been common practice for some time.

Some companies are using sophisticated technology to monitor their employees, to make sure that they don't steal paper clips. Surveillance may also turn into voyeurism. There is a growing incidence of hidden cameras in public showers, toilets, and locker rooms. Peeping Toms now have mobile phones with built-in cameras, which makes it difficult to spot what they are up to. It can easily lead to blackmail.

Some people actively *want* to be exposed to the public gaze. They apply and audition to take part in 'reality TV', which usually involves competing in idiotic and embarrassing tasks. In one programme – actually called Big Brother – twelve participants are put together in a specially constructed house where they live for some weeks, with hidden cameras filming their every move twenty-four hours a day. There is no privacy, even in the loo or shower. The highlights are shown on television. Such shameless exhibitionism is decidedly un-British but it attracts large audiences.

The Government plans to introduce identity cards, a move that is widely regarded as an attempt to strengthen social and political control. The scheme will produce an enormous database holding details of everything from our shopping habits to our medical history. Offices will be set up across Britain to record fingerprints, facial features, and iris scans. The police can then match the photos they have taken with those on the ID system, identifying people who have taken part in demonstrations and see immediately where they live etc. Ministers say that the aim is to protect us against terrorism, but it is far from clear that it will do anything of the sort. The costs are huge and the bureaucratic implications are nightmarish.

When you become a citizen of the United Kingdom you promised, in your oath of allegiance, to "respect its rights and freedoms." You are entitled to demand that the authorities should do the same. One of the rights is to demonstrate peacefully against policies you disagree with. If the police tries to stop you, or an official treats you unfairly, use your camera phone to take pictures of the incident and send them to your member of parliament. One of the MP's most important functions is to act as a watchdog and, fortunately, most are not afraid to bark.

Join a Committee

Your chances of making a successful stand are enhanced if you have the support of others. This may involve drawing up a petition, and collecting as many signatures as possible, but an easier way to join a committee – or, better still, become its chairman.

Committees play a significant role in the democratic process. They, too, like to think of themselves as watchdogs and are generally taken more seriously than individual citizens. They are a very British way of expressing discontent. Some are little more than 'talking shops' – their members spend most of their time arguing with each other and seldom reach any conclusion. They keep minutes which no-one else bothers to read and are reluctant to offend the authorities. But many are a force to be reckoned with. They send stern letters to MP's, councillors, ministers, quangoes, commissions, senior police officers and others who are in a position to *do* something. They all hate negative publicity so copies go to the press; it often turns out to be a useful ally.

If there isn't a committee in your neighbourhood (which is unlikely) you can always start one. Find a few people who share your views: ideally they should include a lawyer or a retired civil servant who knows how Government works. Think up an impressive name, hold regular meetings, and persuade your fellow members that talking is not enough. You will be watched, and listed as a troublemaker, but as chairman of a committee you will be treated with respect.

The Stiff Upper Lip

You have probably heard this strange expression, used nowhere else, and wondered what it means.

The stiff upper lip is a British invention traditionally associated with the aristocracy and people who have been educated in the better public schools. It is, basically, a style of speech in which lip movements are kept to a minimum and jaw movements are barely discernible. This is a trick that speakers of other languages find much more difficult to perform and you are under no obligation to do so. Indeed, it is best not to make the attempt because you run the risk of being regarded as a pretentious 'toff' – an offence not readily forgiven in suburbia.

The expression is also used to describe the ability to bottle up or disguise one's feelings. A stiff upper lip involves maintaining an impassive, serious countenance whatever the circumstances, which is almost impossible for immigrants from countries like Italy, France and Spain. Members of the British upper classes *never* lose their temper, even if greatly provoked, and frown on exuberant displays of emotion. The Earl of Chesterfield once summed it up in a letter to his son. "Having mentioned laughter", he wrote, "I must particularly warn you against it. Frequent and loud laughter is the characteristic of folly and ill manners; it is the manner in which the mob express their silly joy at silly things; and they call it being merry. In my mind there is nothing so ill-bred as audible laughter".

Ill-bred Americans have been known to argue that there is another reason for the British stiff upper lip – to hide bad teeth. This is an outrageous slander which you should not endorse, or repeat, if you wish to be invited to cocktail parties and other social events.

Titles

Many immigrants are bewildered by the formidable array of British titles and other honours. You are no doubt anxious to show proper respect but don't despair if you make a mistake: indigenous Brits often have the same problem. The correct way to introduce, speak, or write to people with handles to their name is a subject of daunting intricacy.

You are unlikely to encounter Black Rod, Gold-stick-in-waiting, or ladies of the Queen's Bedchamber (if you should meet the Queen herself, Ma'am will do nicely). You will, however, need to know how to address Mayors, magistrates, civil servants, and others in an official position because they will take quick offence if you fail to address them properly.

A common source of confusion is whether to write Mr or Esq, or both, in sending a letter. Esquire was defined by medieval law as rank mid-way between knight and gentleman. It later became catch-all for anyone from the right sort of family. Today most of us qualify. It comes at the end of a line but can't be combined with any title or rank that precedes the name. If you are writing to a Lord or Knight, for example, don't use the less important handle.

You can't go wrong with a professional title like doctor – or so you may think. Qualified surgeons prefer to be called Mr, which often leads to erroneous assumption that they are not real doctors.

Knights should be addressed as 'Sir' but it is perfectly in order to use their first name – another quaint British custom. The wife of a knight is called 'Lady' but you should only use her surname. Peers of the realm have different ranks and may have a territorial name in addition to their surname – as in Lord Marshall of Knightsbridge. A Duke is 'Your Grace' but if you speak to someone with a lower rank 'My Lord' is the usual form.

Got that? It gets more complicated. Senior judges are addressed as 'My Lord' or 'Your Lordship', even if they don't have a peerage, and Mayors of cities like Belfast and Cardiff expect to be called 'My Lord Mayor'. (Others are 'Your Worship', which also applies to magistrates, but in Edinburgh and Glasgow the word 'Provost' is used instead of Mayor).

You may also be baffled by the British fondness for honours associated with the Empire. It may be gone, but much effort continues to be expended in the pursuit of appellations like MBE, OBE, and CBE. What, you may ask, does a Commander of the British Empire actually *do*? The short answer is 'nothing'. The honours were invented by a former Prime Minister who needed to raise money and found eager buyers; they have been used since to reward people who have performed some service for the country but who are not considered sufficiently important to merit a knighthood or a peerage. The good news is that, as a new citizen you are permitted to join the pursuit – many immigrants have done so and succeeded. There is also no need to worry that, if you become a knight, you will have to fight dragons, joust, or perform other dangerous acts of chivalry. (Rescuing damsels in distress is optional).

Foreign honours do not have the same status. Aristocratic titles like Count, Graf or Marquis still have some snob value but this has been greatly diminished by the withdrawal of official recognition in republics like France and Italy. The British are not impressed by replacements like *cavaliere* and *commendantore*, which even the Italians don't take seriously. If you already have such a dubious honour you should be aware that

British citizens require written permission from the Her Majesty to wear any foreign insignia in public. It dates back to the days of Queen Elizabeth I, who got so annoyed by the distinctions conferred on her courtiers by scheming foreigners that she decreed: "they are my dogs and they shall wear my collars".

Social Status

The importance attached to titles which imply a superior social position is one of the main reasons why the British are still said to be obsessed with class. This is certainly true of some of us, but you would be wrong to assume that there are borders which you cannot cross. Many people from humble backgrounds have done so. Wealthy pop stars like Mick Jagger, Elton John, and Paul McCartney have been given knighthoods and the once exclusively upper-class set now includes business leaders who left school at 16 and luminaries from the world of fashion.

Immigrants from former colonies sit in the House of Lords and many years have passed since an aristocrat last occupied 10 Downing Street. Margaret Thatcher, the first female prime minister, was the daughter of a grocer. John Major, who succeeded her, went into politics when he could not get a job as a bus conductor. A strong advocate of a 'classless society', he told a parliamentary committee after he left Downing Street that he disapproved of the 'antiquated' honours system and found the habit of seeking titles 'tedious and unattractive'. Since then, however, he has become Sir John, a member of the ancient Order of the Garter.

Founded by King Edward III in 1348, its emblem is a blue and gold ribbon, or garter, worn by men below the left knee and by women on the left arm. It bears the motto Honi soit qui mal y pense – shame on him who thinks ill of it. The current prime minister is still a commoner but it would not be surprising if he, too, eventually accepted the same honour.

The perception that class distinctions continue to play a significant role is based, in part, on films and TV sitcoms about an era in which everyone knew his or her 'place'. But times have clearly changed. The old upper-class has gone through a period of gradual decline. The dukes, marquises, and earls are trying to hang on to their estates, and remain respected members of rural communities, but wealth based on land is not the same as ready cash, which many of them desperately lack. It is difficult to stay aloof, or to show disdain for trade, if one is forced to welcome tourists to one's stately home in order to pay for the upkeep.

In fairness, it must be said that there is less snobbery among genuine aristocrats than among those who aspire to join their ranks. The obsession with social status is a thoroughly middle-class characteristic.

The late Alan Clark was a classic snob. He boasted about his ownership of a castle and famously said about a fellow MP that he was 'the kind of man who buys his own furniture', but failed to gain a senior job in government, or a title, and is best remembered for his sexual exploits and a diary in which he made scathing comments about people he considered to be socially inferior. You will probably meet others like him but don't let them intimidate you.

The old divisions have been eroded in many ways. We are no longer prisoners of our class. Young people from all walks of life go to public schools and study together at universities like Oxford and Cambridge; marriage outside one's class is commonplace; geographic mobility has increased; control of most large companies has shifted from owners to managers; and Thatcherism dealt a massive blow to trade union leaders who passionately believed in the need to engage in relentless conflict with the 'ruling class'. (A Labour minister once explained to me that the words of his party's traditional hymn, the Red Flag, had been changed by some of his constituents to 'the working class can kiss my arse, I've got the foreman's job at last').

We still have more than our share of snobs, but they are just as likely to be found in academic and literary circles than among the old upper-class, and discrimination is nowadays more often based on race and age than on social status.

Some estates have been bought by entrepreneurs who were born and raised in council houses, and by immigrants from Asia. You may have seen the popular TV series, *To The Manor Born*, in which a self-made millionaire of foreign origin tries to deal with the snobbish widow whose family used to own the place. Her patronising attempts to defend 'old values' were amusing but also showed what the *nouveaux riches* are up against.

There are still class distinctions and you may like to know what they are. In general, they are based on indicators such as speech, manner, taste, and lifestyle choices. The way we speak is high on the list; a snob like Professor Henry Higgins (remember *My Fair Lady*?) would still be appalled by the accent of today's Eliza Doolittle and try to change it.

Regional accents have become much more acceptable, but this doesn't apply to London's Cockneys. They use words like 'somefink' and 'nuffink'. Teeth are 'teef'. They say "pardon" (a misguided attempt to sound posh) and call lunch 'dinner'. Bosses are 'guv'. This may not matter if you live in the same environment, but it won't do if you want to be upwardly mobile.

People who consider themselves to be socially superior have a different linguistic code (see also the chapter on Having it Out). They speak what they claim is 'proper' English and often sound absurdly pretentious. They say 'hice' instead of house and use words like 'orf', 'corst' and 'lorst'. Don't worry if you don't understand what they are on about ("shawking withah weir hevving"). Many of us have the same problem. Don't even think of trying to sound like them.

Foreigners are in a different category. A French or Italian accent is generally thought to be charming, but Germans still have a bit of a problem because of the war. Asian accents are associated with trade and the medical profession but are acceptable if, a) you are rich, and b) you respect and seek to emulate your class-conscious fellow citizens.

Some glossy magazines have another way of maintaining class distinctions – they invent new labels for what they claim are homogenous sectors of British society. Most of this is hokum.

You have probably heard about 'Chavs', a pejorative term used to describe a white urban class set apart by a lack of education, fecklessness, and bad taste. The term apparently derives from 'chavi', the Romany word for child, but some have suggested that it's a play on the words 'council house violence'. Chavs include wealthy people like David and Victoria Beckham. They are the upper echelon of Chavdom, with a penchant for flashy jewellery, Caribbean holidays, and second homes abroad. They may be 'dead common' but they tend to have a lot more fun than their snobbish critics.

Urban middle-class people with jobs in the City, or in advertising, used to be known as Yuppies. A more fashionable term is Guppies, which stands for Grown-Up Party People. Guppies are mainly affluent young Londoners who hang out in trendy bars and nightclubs until the early hours. Leading members include royals like Prince William and Prince Harry.

The Government has also come up with a new classification – Neets. It's an acronym for young people aged 16 to 24 'Not in Employment, Education or Training'. There are more than a million of them in Britain and each is said to cost the taxpayers nearly £100,000. Female 'Neets' are single mothers on benefits with lots of babies and multiple partners. They lead unhappy lives, drinking, smoking and eating unhealthily. Male 'Neets' spend much time in prison, find work 'difficult', drink and take drugs, and die of something horrible in their early seventies. Ministers say that 'greater priority' needs to be given to this underclass; youngsters are to be offered a bribe to take full-time education or training.

We can all play this game. I am the founder of IBASA – Independent Brits Against Social Apartheid. Membership is free and open to everyone.

The 'Old Boy Network'

Many of us base our judgements on what kind of school someone went to. We are not talking about foreign schools, which don't count, but about British educational establishments which are reckoned to be superior to the state system. They may not have higher academic standards (though, to be fair, many of them do) but they teach good manners. Rather oddly, we call them public schools. It is misleading because they are private or, to use a more fashionable term, independent.

In earlier days one of the main functions was to produce an elite that could rule the Empire. When that vanished, the objective was to turn out well-spoken young men with the 'right' social credentials. If you went to a school like Eton or Harrow you stood a good chance of being accepted as a bona fide member of the 'Old Boy Network'. Women had their own prestigious colleges, but their primary aim was to teach them how to be supportive wives. Learning how to host a stylish dinner party was considered to be more important than administrative skills.

The City, London's financial district, was like a cosy club. *Who* you knew was more important than *what* you knew. The idea that women might one day become members of the Stock Exchange, or partners in a merchant bank, was regarded as absurd. Men from working class backgrounds had little chance of making it to the boardroom.

All this has changed. The old family firms have been hoovered up into financial supermarkets and aggressively commercial outfits. The English gents who used to run the City chose to sell out to foreigners, who now play the dominant role. There is little room for the cult of the amateur and the affections that tend to accompany it. Brains are more important than class and women are no longer ostracised.

If this is not as widely recognised as it should be, it is partly because the City still keeps up the trappings of a separate existence. Visiting heads of state are entertained in the Guildhall by a Lord Mayor in medieval regalia, flanked by pikemen in uniforms dating back 700 years and each November a new chap gets into an ornate coach and waves to the common folk. The British may work for foreigners but many continue to dress up in robes and chains, symbolising offices that have long ceased to have any real meaning. The *real* Mayor of London is a working class bloke who makes no secret of his contempt for this tomfoolery.

The new professionalism is also very much in evidence outside the City. Most big companies are run by chief executives who are experts in areas like finance and marketing, rather than members of an 'Old Boy Network'. Some are foreigners, which isn't surprising given the change in ownership of British industry. (All the major players in the motor industry are foreign-owned: Ford, Nissan, Toyota, BMW, Honda. Rupert Murdoch, controls three of our most influential newspapers as well as Sky television. Harrods, still widely thought to be a uniquely British institution, is owned by an Egyptian who has been denied citizenship).

Public schools remain popular because many parents want to do 'the best' for their children. An expensive private education, they maintain, is a 'good investment'. There may well be some truth in that, but it is seldom the only reason. Many cannot bear the thought that their offspring may have to mix with children from working-class backgrounds and acquire their vulgar habits. The self-made millionaire

THE 'OLD BOY NETWORK'

does not want his son or daughter to talk and behave like the people in the street where he grew up in. It may happen anyway, if and when they go to university, but he hopes and expects that they will not be unduly influenced.

Not surprisingly, left-wing politicians regard public schools as socially divisive. This, of course, is precisely why so many affluent parents like them. They include immigrants who want their children to have a 'better start' than they had, and foreigners who send their kids to British public schools because they *admire* our class structure. (Many foreign royals make a point of having them educated in Britain, especially if they have a military career in mind. Sandhurst is widely regarded as the world's best academy for potential officers. Its tough instructors have little respect for their illustrious recruits. The late King Hussein of Jordan liked to tell what happened when he displeased a sergeant major. "You, Sir, are a 'orrible little king", he was told).

It is plainly up to you to make up your own mind about all this. The cost is an obvious factor – fees are high and, remember, you will have to fork out a lot more if your child later goes to a university.

A third of Britain's teenagers leave schools at 16 without a qualification. All they have to show for their time there is the ability to read, write, and do sums. Others manage to gain a place at one of the universities: state-educated students now account for 68 per cent of new admissions.

A degree is still useful and, in some fields, essential. But many people have done well without it. Philip Green, the high street retailer, left school at 15 to join the rag trade and become a billionaire. Sir Alan Sugar, founder of the home electronics firm, Amstrad, left at 16. Sir

Richard Branson walked away from his public school, Stowe, because he was eager to try his luck in publishing. (His first venture, ironically, was a magazine called *Student*. It flopped but he says that the experience taught him more than he could have learned at Stowe or university: as we all know, he later became a byword for entrepreneurial flair).

There are, today, so many graduates that finding a job takes much longer; the red carpet that used to greet young men and women with academic credentials has gone. When my son decided to leave school at 16 I asked him what he wanted to do. He said that he liked the idea of becoming a chef. He was trained at the Savoy Hotel in London. I gladly supported him for three years and was proud when he gained his diploma.

The Government says that Britain has a wide-ranging skills shortage. It isn't going to be remedied by sending every teenager to university, where three years may be devoted to studying history or the classics. Modern apprenticeships are the key to providing chefs, electricians, plumbers, car mechanics, and others whose skills are badly needed. This is one of the biggest challenges: are we ready to abandon the deeply ingrained prejudice against 'working class' occupations? The Government believes that it is vital to do so, and is actively seeking to promote vocational training.

I have always believed that parents should seek to establish what their children *want* to do and help them to make the most of whatever talent they may have. Snobbery shouldn't come into it, but we have some way to go before it ceases to be a factor in the vaunted British way of life.

The Name Game

Names are also important in what remains of our class structure. 'Common' English people give their children first names like Sharon, Les, Mavis, and Dave. The 'better sort' prefer Jessica, Hugh, Emma, and Rupert. (Scots like Kirstie, Fiona and James).

The royals caused some confusion with their choice of William for the next-but-one-king and Harry for his brother. They are not considered top-drawer names and snobs thought it was a quite uneccessary attempt to please the working class.

You are, of course, entitles to call your own children whatever you like. But please don't saddle them with poncy names like Lancelot, Torquile, Peregine, or Amber. Stay away from fads and gimmicks.

Names are far more then mere identity tags. They play a significant role in the way we perceive ourselves and in how others see us. Some trigger a positive response; others are associated with negative qualities. This is well understood in showbiz. Hollywood wouldn't have recognised a film star called Issur Danielovitch, so he became Kirk Douglas. Judy Garland started out as Frances Gumm, Tony Curtis as Bernie Schwartz, John Wayne as Marion Morrison, Michael Caine as Maurice Micklewhite, and Woody Allen as Allen Konigsberg. (The movie mogul Sam Goldwyn, born Gelbfish, took a keen interest in the game. He complained when a friend told him the name he had given to his son. "Now why did you call him John?" Goldwyn asked. "Every Tom, Dick and Harry is called John").

Many immigrants change their name completely, from stem to stern, when they become British citizens. Some want to disguise their foreign origins or simply make their name easier to pronounce and spell. Others do so because they think it will help them at work.

When I came to Britain I was Gunter Wilhelm Keese. This too was German, so Wilhelm became William and I adopted my stepfather's surname, Davis. If I had known at the time that I would earn my living as a writer and broadcaster I would have chosen one that was more authorative and eye-catching.

Thousands of British-born people have also changed their name – not counting those who have done so through marriage. In many cases, the principal objective has been to revamp their image. An English friend of mine was so unhappy with his prosaic name, Fred Smith, that he decided to call himself Mark Barrymore. He says that it made him feel better about himself and has been good for his career.

Not everyone goes that far. Some Smiths have more emphasis on their first and middle names (as in Ian Duncan Smith) or changed the spelling to Smythe. Others have simply added another surname (as in Smith-Hamilton) because hyphens imply an upper class background. The law takes a tolerant view of changes, so long as there is no fraudulent or criminal intent and you use your new name consistently.

You may, after you have assessed all the factors, be perfectly content with the one you have. You are certainly not obliged to drop it. Many immigrants have done well despite their foreign name. (Lakshmi Mittal for example, has become one of the richest men in Britain). There is no doubt, however, that a positive and British-sounding name can make a difference, not only to your social standing but also in business and in your personal relationships.

The Season

When people like Les and Dave talk about 'the season' they usually have football in mind. For Jessica, Hugh and others who consider themselves to be superior it means a potpourri of unmissable social events – Ascot, the Derby, the Henley Regatta, Cowes Week on the Isle of Wight, the Braemar Royal Highland Gathering, the patriotic fervour of the last night of the proms in London's Albert Hall, charity balls and country house parties.

Much of this can nowadays be seen on television, but what matters is *being* there. Corporations hire marquees, boxes, and the best seats so that they can entertain their clients in style. Car dealers, property developers, designers, advertising executives, merchant bankers and others engaged in 'trade' find it advantageous to do the same – or at least to turn up so that they can make new contacts. Affluent Americans, Arab sheiks, and the nouveau riches of countries like India come because they want to be part of the British social scene. Showbiz celebrities (and would-be celebrities) attend because they love to be recognised and flattered.

A highlight of the season is Ladies Day at Ascot. The racing is not important: this is an opportunity to display the latest creations of leading fashion designers. Some women go to extraordinary lengths to get attention. Hats, in particular, tend to be remarkable concoctions, ranging from the over the top to the totally outrageous.

Henley's Royal Regatta is another occasion when the social side threatens to overtake the sport. Marquees blossom out on the river bank, men wear blazers and boaters, and copious quantities of champagne and Pimms are consumed along with smoked salmon and strawberries.

At the Glyndebourne Opera Festival. which has become one of the most prestigious events, there is a strict dress code: black tie is essential. Champagne corks are popped in the garden before everyone troops into the state-of-the-art opera house to see the latest production of Mozart's *Magic Flute*. Picnics are also very much in evidence.

Invitations to charity balls and country house parties are much sought after but hard to come by unless the organisers, or hosts, feel that you *belong* – one of the unwritten rules based to a large extent on your background and connections.

The season inspires an astonishing amount of puritanical vitriol. Left-wing politicians and other members of the dwindling band of class warriors can't bear the thought of people paying a lot of money for what they regard as ego trips and the frivolous pursuit of pleasure. They angrily denounce the evil of toffs, snobs, and elitists getting out their gladrags and having a good time. Some of the hats at Ascot cost as much as a factory worker earns in a month: Glyndebourne charges as much as £150 for a ticket; and have you seen the price of those lavish picnic hampers at Fortnum and Mason?

The 'toffs' ignore them or point out that, by God, Britain is a free country and they are entitled to spend their money in any way they damn well like.

I have never cared for all the social upmanship, but I don't share the indignation of the critics. There are plenty of events which are open to people with modest means. The Edinburgh Festival is a splendid annual showcase for new talent, including subversive comedians. Glastonbury has become famous as a boisterous hippy festival, featuring bands with names like the Killers, Futureheads, White Stripes, Hot Hot Heat, Deadbeats, and the Peoples Republic of Disco. Brighton has the biggest arts festival in England, drawing performers from all over the world. It is very much rooted in the local community; events include a spectacular procession of 4,000 children from 70 schools, all decked out in fancy dress and marching to the beat of samba bands. Wales has the Eistedfod, dedicated to encouraging and preserving Welsh culture. The Notting Hill Carnival is a jolly romp reflecting London's ethnic diversity, and there are numerous other street parties in towns and villages which are great fun.

Dress Sense

The way we dress says a lot about us, but there are fewer rules than in the past. If you want to participate in 'The Season' you clearly need to know what is expected. For the 'better sort' clothes are a badge of belonging; they make a social statement. You would, however, look silly if you went to a rock festival or a street party in a dinner jacket. For many Brits, especially the young, dress is all about individual self-expression.

It was all very different when I came to Britain as an immigrant, more than fifty years ago. People from working class backgrounds like mine were more willing to conform. They did not have 'ideas above their station' and it wasn't done to 'make an exhibition of yourself'.

In the City, where I started work as an office boy, gents wore a bowler hat, white shirt, dark suit, and a regimental or old school tie. They always carried a furled umbrella, even on sunny days. I did not qualify for their exalted status but had to dress in what the manager called 'an appropriate matter'. I was rebuked when I wore brown shoes and incurred his displeasure again when, a week later, I turned up in a blue shirt. "You look", he thundered, "like a ship's engineer on a Sunday outing".

Today such stuffy attitudes would be regarded as absurd. There is no longer an 'establishment uniform'. Suits still predominate, but bowler hats have vanished and no-one cares about the colour of one's shoes or shirt. Many firms not only allow their employees to wear their own choice of clothes but have imported the American custom of 'dressing down' on Fridays.

Sartorial permissiveness began in the 1960's because young people decided to rebel against the rules laid down by the older generation. We wallowed in the bright colours and inventive designs introduced by new heroes like Mary Quant. Men, they told us, did not have to dress like Dad and Uncle Norman. Women did not have to look like Mum and Auntie Flo.

For me, as for many others of my age and background, Carnaby Street became the centre of the fashion globe. We bought our gear there because it was affordable and daring. It may not seem a big deal now that so many high street shops and boutiques sell glamorous clothes (and even Marks & Spencer has been forced to change course) but at the time it was heady stuff – we felt like revolutionaries.

The 'better sort' were appalled, which made it all the more exciting. Some have been complaining about 'the decline in standards' ever since. Here is what one member of the House of Lords wrote about it in a society journal:

"We have progressively collapsed into a wasteland of grubby blue jeans, sweat shirts and trainers. One of the abiding symbols of the age will undoubtedly be the image of a young man dressed like a garbage collector, with a can of soft drink in one hand, a hamburger in the other, and a three-day growth of beard on his face".

Others say they are disgruntled by the 'vulgarity' of the nouveaux riches, the exhibitionism of pop stars and other celebrities, and the sight of women in business suits. Men are wearing bracelets and diamond earrings! It's all in such frightfully bad taste.

Some dress codes have more to do with religion than with class. This is certainly true of communities with a high percentage of Muslims, Sikhs and Hindus. They feel entitled to make their own rules. This, too, upsets many Brits. You are no doubt familiar with their arguments: it leads to a ghetto mentality, intensifies differences, encourages misunderstanding, and so on. Immigrants, they insist, must make an effort to integrate.

Yes, but many of these fellow citizens were born in Britain or are the children of immigrants. They don't approve of the way *we* dress but don't presume to lecture us.

Early in 2004 a High Court judge had to decide whether a school in Luton could force a teenage pupil to wear its uniform. The teenager, a Muslim girl, complained that the headmaster was "eroding her human rights". She had been sent home for wearing a jilbab, an ankle-length dress that leaves only the face and hands visible. She would not go back unless the rule was changed. The judge, who knew that she was being used by extremist pressure groups, threw out the case. Other Muslims welcomed the verdict because, they said, it was the wrong kind of fight. Religious beliefs were important but school regulations were there for the benefit of all the pupils and should be respected. If the jilbab were allowed then it would also be reasonable to let Jewish boys have curled forelocks and fringed shawls and to permit Bhuddists to wear robes.

A fair point, but the girl and her brother decided to contest the High Court ruling. In March 2005 the Court of Appeal overturned the earlier verdict. Lord Justice Brooke said that she had been 'denied the right to education and to manifest her religious beliefs' when the school had sent her home.

This whole issue of dress codes is bound to remain controversial. The Scots have the kilt but are not obliged to wear it – few do so, except on special occasions. The English don't have a 'national costume' and there is no law which says we must all look alike. (Even his Lordship would object to any attempt to turn us into a nation of Star Trek characters). There is no doubt, however, that the way we dress has a considerable influence on how we are perceived by others. Appearance still matters – a fact of British life that is well understood by politicians, advertising executives, showbiz personalities, car dealers, estate agents, and insurance salesmen who will tell you that dress sense is all about making a 'good impression'.

Greetings

Never on the mouth.

Jensen

When you are introduced to someone for the first time he or she may say "How do you do?" This is simply a polite form of greeting: you are not expected to embark on a lengthy explanation of your current state of health. The correct response is to repeat the question back: "How do you do?"

Once you get to know each other better, it may be changed to "how are you?" You should say "fine", even if you feel lousy. Anything else may lead to a prolonged and tiresome discussion of your respective ailments.

Another popular form of ritual greeting is to comment on the weather. It is a very British way of 'breaking the ice', though ice is one of the few things we seldom see. There is a wide range of options because the weather changes constantly. "Nasty out, isn't it?" may be followed later in the same day by "Nice to see the sun again, eh?" The questions require some response, but here again there is no need to go into detail. The key point is to keep in mind that you should never contradict anybody – it is considered rude to do so. The safest course is to express agreement, but you are permitted to add some comment of your own. If you are told that it's 'freezing', you should say "Yes, but at least it's not raining". If it rains you may reply: "Yes, but the forecasters are predicting better weather for tomorrow".

In recent years it has also become fashionable – at least in England – to adopt foreign habits like shaking hands, hugging, and kissing. A handshake is intended to be an expression of solidarity, mostly used by men, but onc that crushes the fingers is aggressive, not friendly, and a limp hand is no good at all.

Heterosexual British males don't embrace each other as readily as Latins do, and although this is changing you should avoid the bear-hug which was so popular in Eastern Europe during the communist era. Women are more likely to use an embrace as a demonstration of affection and goodwill, but over-enthusiastic hugging of males other than one's husband or boyfriend is liable to be misinterpreted.

This also applied to kissing. The rules are less strict than in the past – women are more inclined these days to kiss friends and acquaintances of both sexes – but there are still limits. The standard British social kiss involves pecking each other on the cheek. (Your mouth may not actually touch the other person's cheek – a smack in the air will suffice). Noisy suctions and exuberant exclamations are un-British. You should *never* put lips to lips.

There is still some confusion about how many times one should kiss, and whether one should begin on the left or right, but this is in the process of being sorted out. Kissing a woman's hand is regarded as antiquated and best left to Austrian counts.

Bear in mind that young people tend to be more boisterous in their greetings than the older generation, especially if they work in fields like journalism, advertising, the theatre, fashion, and pop music. If you don't wish to be embraced or kissed, or have doubts about the wisdom of such intimate contact, make sure you keep at a safe distance.

Another issue you need to consider is the use of first names. This was long thought to be impolite until one had established a close relationship but many of us have been influenced by American informality and it is now quite common to address people one had just met by their given name. The risk is that you will seem presumptuous, so it is generally a good idea to wait until the other person has initiated the process.

Some of us have nicknames, which may be collective (The English, for example, often refer to Scots as 'Jock' or 'Mac') or personal. The latter were usually acquired at school and are likely to be regarded as offensive by the person at whom they are directed.

You should also familiarise yourself with the British way of saying goodbye. Kissing is not obligatory but, like the handshake, has become accepted practice. "It was nice to meet you" will generally do if you are parting from people to whom you have recently been introduced. If you are visiting someone's home, allow at least 10 minutes from the initial goodbye to your actual departure and remember to say that you had a 'lovely time', even if you have been bored stiff by the conversation. It is impolite to give the impression that one is desperate to leave.

The American habit of telling people to "have a nice day" hasn't caught on in Britain, mainly because it seems insincere – and usually is. The late Sir Peter Ustinov once shot back with "thank you, but I have other plans". Americans may have found this rude, but the British applauded his wit.

Tipping Points

Another aspect of social behaviour you need to be familiar with is tipping. This is a minefield because there are no fixed rules. It is even more difficult for foreigners because customs vary from country to country. In America, tipping is endemic and often done to excess. The British tend to be more stingy.

Some people say that they find the whole business embarrassing: they cringe at the condescension implicit in the tip. Isn't it humiliating for the taxi driver, hairdresser, or barber to be given money on top of the fee they charge? No, is the answer. You are not, however, expected to tip shop assistants, doctors, nurses, pilots and cabin crew, bus conductors, petrol pump attendants and authors.

Tipping is really about thanking and if you focus on that it's easier to handle. Don't worry about getting the amount wrong; they are used to variations. Ten per cent is usually regarded as a minimum but no-one will complain if you are more generous.

Confusion reigns in restaurants because some include a service charge in the bill while others leave it to their customers to decide how much to tip. The charge is supposed to be optional, and you can ask to have it removed if you are unhappy, but most of us pay it anyway because we hate to make a fuss. We even leave a little extra for the waiter because we feel sorry for him.

The cost will inevitably be higher if you go to an expensive restaurant rather than to McDonalds or Pizza Express. You not only have to fork out a sizeable 'gratuity' but also tip the people who take your coat, carve your beef, run a basin of tepid water for you in the lavatory, and hail you a taxi. This is especially important if you intend to become a regular customer; they *never* forget someone who has been mean and have ways of taking revenge.

Business executives with lavish expense accounts sometimes tip the maitre d' as soon as they arrive. This is intended as a bribe – the aim is to jump the queue and get the best table in the room. It should be done discreetly: the usual method is to fold the note flat in your palm and pretend to be shaking his hand.

Tipping gets even more complex if you stay in a top hotel because all sorts of other people expect to be 'looked after' – the chambermaid, concierge, luggage porter, lift attendant, room service waiter, bartender, doorman, and so on.

If a rich couple invite you to spend the weekend with them you should tip the butler, maid, cook, chauffeur, or any other member of the staff who has taken care of you. If it's a shooting weekend you will also have to pay your loader £50 a day and your keeper the going rate for every 100 birds shot.

You may, of course, be quite happy to stay at home and make occasional forays to your local pizza restaurant or pub. Most of us can't afford to do much else. But there is one time of the year when it is absolutely vital to tip as generously as possible: Christmas. The people who have collected your rubbish, or delivered your newspapers, expect a financial reward and will be upset if you are stingy or, worse, ignore them. The 'Christmas Box' is a British tradition which needs to be upheld if you want good service in the coming year.

What if you are the one who collects the rubbish and delivers the papers? How can you ensure that your work will be rewarded? The obvious answer is to knock on every door and ask for a tip. Some people do just that, but many prefer a more subtle approach. They pop a Christmas card or calendar through the letter box and hope that the recipient will get the message. They wait for a few days and *then* knock on doors.

Do *not* tell them about your financial problems because you may get a lecture on the importance of staying out of debt or a lengthy account of the resident's own difficulties. And avoid whatever temptation there may be to threaten retribution if they don't come across: your boss is bound to hear about it.

Tipping is not a science. It is an art, and a very delicate art. The word 'tip' is said to come from 18th century England, where cafés used to feature a little box by the door with 'To Insure Promptitude' written on the side. Such boxes are nowadays found mainly in churches, but without any guarantees. You may feel that it should not be necessary to bribe anyone, but that is widely considered to be a naïve view of Britain in the 21st century.

Good Sports

You may also have heard it said about a friend or acquaintance that he or she is a 'good sport'. You need to understand what this means.

A good sport is not someone who *wins* but a player who knows how to lose without throwing a tantrum. It was an Englishman who decreed that "it matters not who won or lost, but how you played the game". Cynics say this is simply a convenient excuse and it is certainly not a view shared by today's football fans, who are more likely to agree with the dictum laid down by another Englishman, George Orwell, that "football is war without shooting". (They have their own list of excuses, such as "the referee was blind" and "the other side cheated").

Accepting defeat with dignity has long been associated with gentlemanly sports like cricket, tennis, golf, and polo. Unfortunately the modern emphasis on professionalism and the behaviour of foreigners who are obsessed with winning has led many of us to change our attitude. We still have players who know how to lose without shouting abuse at umpires but the younger generation has become more aggressive. This is particularly true of people who have not been educated at a decent public school, like Eton.

As a new citizen you should demonstrate your loyalty be applauding British players, even if you are disappointed by their performance, but it is not necessary to drape yourself in the national flag. Never boo at a cricket match: it would be seen as evidence that you have not yet become fully integrated.

The Scots have Highland Games, at which they toss roughly trimmed pine trunks in all directions – an atavistic custom which the English find puzzling and should not be attempted unless you are seven feet tall, weigh 20 stone, and wear a skirt. A good sport is a tosser who apologises for not being able to lift the trunk.

If you are invited to join in a game of tennis or golf, and lose, remember to tell your opponent how sorry you are that you have not managed to do better. This also applies if you take part in an egg-and-spoon race.

Cheating at *any* sport is bad form and should not be contemplated unless you are absolutely sure that you can get away with it.

Standing In Line

It is important to learn how to queue. The Latin disdain for queues never ceases to dismay the British, to whom it seems thoroughly uncivilised. As a new citizen you must abandon whatever reservations you may have had in the past about standing in line.

Anthropologists have come up with several explanations for this practice of queueing, which we invented. The most plausible is a compulsive need for orderliness, shared with other Anglo-Saxons. Predictability is essential – when we join a queue we know what to expect and can tell how we stand in relation to everyone else. We are quite content to form disciplined lines at ticket counters, bus stops, taxi ranks, airline check-ins, and supermarket check-outs providing that others do not try and steal an advantage. There are even occasions when people who are about to be served forgo their turn by pointing out that someone else has arrived before them – a form of self-denial which the Latins find incomprehensible.

If someone (probably a foreigner or a rock star) pushes ahead of you don't even hint that he or she did it on purpose. The correct procedure is to say "excuse me, I was here first" and to remind the offender that "there is a queue". It is, however, permissible to switch to a shorter queue or, if a new counter opens, to form your own. This may seem inconsistent, but there is no need to apologise. Just remember not to gloat.

There is another exception to the rules. If you go to the theatre you will find the jostle of people ordering drinks during the interval resembles a rugby scrum. Even the British have not yet found a way of dealing with this blatant transgression of the cherished principle of 'fair play'.

On The Road

The biggest queues are often encountered on roads and motorways, where the same rules are supposed to apply. We are accustomed to bumper-to-bumper traffic, especially on Bank Holidays, and tend to be rather phlegmatic and philosophical about being held up for hours.

Unfortunately some of our young people have acquired foreign habits along with their Porsches, BMW's, Ferraris, and Mercedes sports cars. Their impatient style of driving is considered un-British and you should resist the temptation to behave in a similar manner if you wish to be fully integrated.

We find traffic jams just as frustrating as the French and Italians but, unlike them, the majority of British drivers do not regard traffic laws as flexible guidelines. We also take a dim view of insults and hand signals that are not in the Highway Code. Aggressive tactics are liable to lead to what has become known as 'road rage' – you risk being punched on the nose by someone who is bigger and stronger than you. Our hospitals are already overcrowded.

It is bad form to jump a queue, honk your horn (usually a futile gesture) or go through an intersection after the traffic lights have turned red (a privilege reserved for cyclists). Speeding will also get you into trouble. No-one is immune, not even royalty. Princess Anne was stopped by the police, and later fined in court, when she exceeded the speed limit near her home – proof, it was pointed out by the magistrates, that when it comes to driving everyone is equal under the law. Don't imagine that you can get away with excuses. The police have heard them all before and attempts to argue with an officer are guaranteed to make him more determined to punish you.

Another aspect which you would do well to study, and come to terms with, is parking. Forget whatever practice you may have been used to before coming to Britain – few things are more likely to alienate your new fellow-citizens than parking on yellow lines or in spaces allocated to local residents and disabled drivers. Make no mistake: we will not hesitate to denounce you to traffic wardens if you ignore the rules.

Punctuality

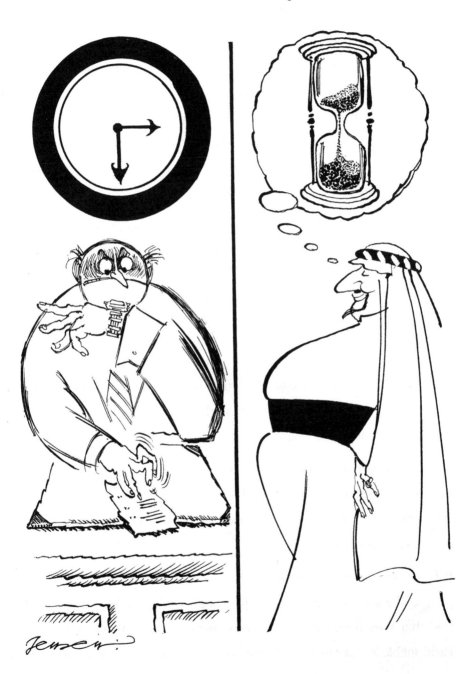

One of the problems with all this is that it may make you late for an appointment. A few minutes don't matter, but half an hour certainly does.

Concern with time-keeping is another British tradition which puzzled many foreigners – especially Spaniards, Greeks, South Americans and Arabs. They are used to a more casual approach and find it hard to understand why we are so obsessed with schedules and deadlines, which they regard as artificial and unnecessary. Why do Anglo-Saxons have this need to hurry through life?

A Spaniard or Arab, when he arrives an hour late, might mumble something which resembles an explanation. He had something else to take care of first. Or he met a friend along the way who invited him for a cup of coffee and it would have been impolite to refuse. Why make a fuss?

Such behaviour may be acceptable – just – if the foreigner is a visitor to our shores. One has to make allowances. It is *not* acceptable if you are an immigrant who has been granted British citizenship. You are expected to know the rules.

Being late is generally regarded as a sign of disorganisation or rudeness. Yes, we know that you may have had to queue, or that you may have been caught in a traffic jam, but you should have taken that into account before leaving home.

It is particularly important not to be late for appointments with busy people like doctors, dentists, and potential employers. You are liable to find that they have moved on to the next person on their schedule. Fashionable restaurants, too, have little patience with tardy customers:

your table will have gone to someone else and you will have to wait or may be asked to come back another day.

"Better to be three hours too soon than a minute too late", Shakespeare had one of his characters say in the *Merry Wives of Windsor*. A jest, but most of us would agree that being early for an appointment is better. You can always occupy yourself by reading a magazine or, if you are there on business, pretending to be engrossed in the *Financial Times*. If that isn't convenient, aim to be exactly on time.

The rules for social occasions tend to be more flexible. If you are invited to a cocktail party, for example, it isn't necessary to be punctual. The same usually goes for dinner invitations but there are limits. It is bad form to keep your hosts waiting for more than 30 minutes. They've gone to a lot of trouble to please you – cooking your food, uncorking the wine, making sure that you are in congenial company – and you won't be asked again if you behave like one of the foreign blighters who think they can turn up whenever they want. (Arriving too early is not a good idea either, because they may still be in the shower or busy in the kitchen).

If *you* are the host, be specific about what you expect from your guests. Confusion can be avoided by sending a polite note in advance, asking them to come at a certain time – say 7.30pm and 8pm.

There are, of course, exceptions to all of this. If you visit other countries, you must play by their rules. Some 'ethnic communities' may also have different standards. But if you wish to be accepted as truly British – one of us – you should make a serious effort to understand how we feel about time. Punctuality is a virtue; lateness (deliberate or otherwise) is inconsiderate, selfish, and liable to turn potential friends against you. Britain is a tolerant society, but there are some things which are simply *not done.*

No Litter, Please

The Government expects every citizen to keep Britain tidy.

When Margaret Thatcher was prime minister she tried to set an example by marching into London's St James's park to pick up litter. The media said it was a stunt – the litter had apparently been placed there by her aides, who then invited photographers to record this historic initiative. Her efforts were, nevertheless, given extensive publicity.

The current prime minister has not, it seems, managed to find time for a similar excursion but he also wants us to take care of our environment. Unfortunately, many people feel entitled to dispose of their rubbish in any way they like. Britain has become a throw-away society. Many streets are filthy and our parks are spoiled by careless behaviour: families go on picnics and leave their junk behind – plastic bottles, cartons, wrappers, cans, broken toys, newspapers, half-eaten food. The same happens to our beaches in the summer months.

We tend to blame teenage 'louts', but many adults are just as guilty. There is an all too common view that others should clean up after us. They do, of course. Local authorities collect tons of garbage every day. (Older readers will no doubt recall the year when the unions called a strike and mountains of black plastic bags filled with rubbish were left to rot. It was a shocking sight and played a key role in the subsequent downfall of the Government).

You are not required to emulate Lady Thatcher, who armed herself with a fearsome spear and angrily stabbed all the rubbish left in her path. (The police might not accept that you are only doing your civic duty).

What is essential is that you leave public places as you would like to find them. If you see others behaving badly, tell them that you don't want to see this great country of ours turned into a slum. And – a personal plea – don't allow your dog to shit on pavements. Your fellow citizens don't want to have to navigate their way around turds.

Keeping Britain tidy is not just about appearances. Filth also creates health problems. Your adored pet may rummage around in garbage and come home happy but loaded with germs. Restaurants may have an attractive decor but a dirty kitchen. Homes may look neat from the outside but be a disgusting tip behind the smart front door.

Which brings me to another aspect – personal hygiene. The British have long prided themselves on being superior to other nations in cleanliness, but this is a spurious claim. Historians have pointed out that Queen Elizabeth I bathed only once a month, and that in the 18th century it was widely thought that water represented a danger to health. Soap did not come into general use until 1824, and research conducted as late as the 1950s showed that 20 per cent of Londoners *never* took a bath, partly because only one in three houses at the time actually had one. Today they are commonplace, but new research has shown that foreigners like the Japanese and the Americans tend to make greater use of baths and showers. Many of us neglect to wash our hands as often as we should, which may cause infections. (Cold viruses, for example, can be spread through handshakes). Some people even fail to mask their body odours by using deodorants, which is particularly annoying if one has to stand next to them in a crowded train. Do, *please*, try to smell nice.

The Government has taken many steps to protect and preserve the environment. Persistent offenders are liable to be fined. Restaurants which do not meet the standards laid down by inspectors may be forced to close. Builders and others who dump waste illegally may be sent to prison. Hooligans who think it's OK to cover walls with graffiti also risk prosecution. But what is really needed is a change in attitudes. If we don't want Britain to become a slum we need to adopt better habits. This should certainly be on the curriculum of every citizenship class.

Eating Dogs Is Wrong

The British love animals and vigorously defend their rights. They are outraged by the barbarous Canadian habit of clubbing seals to death and will readily join in campaigns to save whales, rhinos, tigers, and endangered butterflies.

Many of us also took part in a valiant battle to prevent foxes being hunted down by men in pink coats. We are still struggling to protect pheasants against people in tweed suits and knee-socks who, apparently, have an insatiable urge to shoot defenceless birds. Unfortunately some of our fellow citizens have not yet been persuaded that they should abandon this distressing pastime. (Immigrants would be well advised not to take sides until the matter is resolved).

You may wonder why we have no objection to the killing of chickens, ducks, rabbits, pigs, cows, sheep, turkeys, salmon, trout, and other fish. The paradox is easily explained. Most of us live in cities and have never seen them killed, let alone participated in the slaughter. They are *products* we buy in supermarkets. Pigs are 'ham' or 'pork', and cows are 'steaks' or 'Sunday joints'. A chicken or lamb is not an animal but *lunch*.

Unlike the French we don't eat horses and we were appalled by reports that Koreans eat dogs. The very idea that Fido or Spot might end up on a menu is too ghastly to contemplate; the British are more civilised.

Dogs and cats occupy a special place in our affections. They are family. Well-bred, well-groomed, and obedient canines are proudly displayed at that great British annual event, Cruft's. (Many children also have an inexplicable fondness for hamsters, frogs and snakes but they would never think of asking Mum to cook them).

Market research has shown that we spend more than £400 million a year on treats, toys, and healthcare for our four-legged and furry friends. Designer toiletries have become a 'must have' accessory. Colognes make pets smell nicer and aromatherapy candles help them to unwind. Other top sellers include a wide range of educational toys, with flashing lights and noises that entertain them while we are out. Balls and frisbees, expensive designer collars and slimming foods are also popular.

Harrods, the posh London store, has an annual pet-a-porter fashion show. Pooches sashay down a luminous pink runway, modelling the latest collections by Burberry, Aquascutum, and Playboy.

Affluent dog-lovers can buy anything from from raincoats to tiaras. The manager of the pet department says that his clients have a maternal relationship with their dogs and see no reason why they should not look as 'fabulous' as their owners.

Other companies offer amenities like a pet gym, a limousine pick-up service, dog yoga workshops, and a spa. There are personal trainers, hairdressers, dog walkers, and even canine psychiatrists. You can also send your pooch to a health farm.

When our playmates die, many of us decide to bury them in the garden and buy a nice coffin and headstone. Pet cemeteries are in decline, because of licensing changes, but firms like Dignity pet Crematorium in Hampshire understand our grief and can be relied upon to treat the darlings with respect. There is a wide choice of urns and one company,

Poffins, does ashes pendants "so that you can have your pet's ashes with you wherever you go".

Daft? Yes, but also rather sad because it says a lot about the state of human relationships. Dogs and cats provide the kind of uncomplicated friendship that the rich often find hard to get elsewhere. It is perhaps not surprising that some leave fortunes to them, much to the annoyance of relatives who usually challenge such bequests on the grounds that they were of 'unsound mind' when they made their will. Judges, who probably have dogs themselves, expect convincing evidence but the usual outcome is a compromise: the relatives promise to take good care of Fido if they get the loot. Fido, of course, is not asked what kind of lifestyle would be acceptable.

A more tricky problem arises when a couple decide to get divorced and have to agree on who gets custody of the pet. For some of us this is a more serious matter than money (we can always make more) or even the future of our children. We cannot bear to be parted from our affectionate and loyal companion and will, if necessary, hire expensive lawyers to argue our case in court. Koreans may regard this as absurd, but it's the British way of settling such an important issue.

Politicians are generally reluctant to get involved in the constant (and often nasty) debate about animal rights but they accept that it can't be ignored if they want to keep their jobs. The House of Commons voted in 2004 to ban hunting with dogs but the Government intends to do much more. A new Animal Welfare Bill will extend a 'duty of care' to all vertebrate animals that are permanently domesticated or in human charge. Goldfish will be banned as fairground prizes, tail-docking of dogs will be halted in most circumstances, and children under 16 will be prohibited from buying pets. It will also be an offence to keep your pet locked in a car on sunny days. People who are convicted of failing in their duty may be disqualified from owning animals.

You may well be tempted to mount a campaign against such meddling and, of course, as a British citizen you are entitled to do so. But watch out if you plan to hand out leaflets dressed as a chicken. Chief police officers have warned protesters who pull off publicity stunts that they run the risk of being mistaken for terrorists.

Mobile Etiquette

Mobile phone are a terrific invention, but the human aspect is troublesome. Many users have a maddening tendency to conduct long monologues in public – on a train or bus, in shops and restaurants, and even in cinemas. They show a total disregard for their fellow-citizens, which many of us regard as frightfully un-British. We don't want to hear about their deals and rivals, or about their complex love life.

One way of stopping them in their tracks is to take out a notebook and start to write things down, looking as if you are interested. It will make them wonder if you are a detective, tax inspector, member of the intelligence service, or gossip columnist.

The ability to speak any time and anywhere puts a considerable strain on the conventions of a system of manners which has evolved in more stationary times. The etiquette danger in mobiles lies in their very efficiency: they work so well in all circumstances that too many people are often tempted to make calls before their brain is engaged. They get upset by one thing or another and instantly vent their anger on the phone – a habit they later regret. Some are mobile bores who have nothing to say but insist on calling anyway – and then going on at inordinate length.

The worst offenders are chatterboxes who go to a restaurant and spend the entire lunch or dinner with a mobile glued to their ear. They not only offend other diners but are guilty of insufferable rudeness towards their own guest, or host, who has to sit there, fuming, while the transgressor blithely chats to absent colleagues or friends. The implication is clear: "you are not significant enough to require my full attention". The obvious answer is to leave him (or her) to it.

This passion for endless blather can also create problems for those at the receiving end. If you are in a meeting, taking a string of calls is bound to annoy others in the same room, and in any case you may not wish to have your conversation overheard. You can pop out for a while but that, too, can become an irritating habit and you may miss an important point or decision. The safest course is to switch off your mobile until the meeting is over.

There are now phones which enable us to see as well as hear the people we are talking to. This carries additional risks. You may be caught in your bathroom, bleary-eyed and unshaven, which is bound to create an unfavourable impression. (Women may be tempted to take a call before they have applied their make-up, which is just as bad). It is also much harder to get away with telling fibs if the caller can look at you in close-up when you are doing it.

Mobile etiquette may seem old-fashioned (ask any teenager)but there is no need to apologise for civilised behaviour. The mobile is not a toy, fashion accessory, status symbol, or a licence to bore. Abraham Lincoln famously said that "it's better to remain silent and be thought a fool than to speak out and remove all doubt". A message worth passing on to the kids.

The Net Catch

Many of us also make extensive use of the Internet. Everyday email has been around for more than a decade, and is a convenient way of communicating with others, but some people have the same tendency to overdo it. They bombard their friends with trivia or fire off messages without considering the effect they may have.

Here is a common scenario. You get an annoying email and, hopping mad, decide to respond immediately. The words flow quickly until you finally hit the last exclamation mark and, with great satisfaction, punch the send button. "That'll show him", you think to yourself. Five minutes later, feeling much calmer now, you read the missive again and realise that it was way over the top. Unfortunately, you can't retrieve it. The damage has been done.

Email sent to colleagues at work can also get you into trouble because it may be seen by people who don't like you or who are rivals. Some have led to charges of sexual harassment; others have cost indiscreet executives their job.

Another dangerous temptation is to respond to Spam, the online version of junk mail. It's intrusive and irritating, and can clog up your in-box with emails about products and services you have no interest in. A prompt response confirms that your address is valid and you will receive more of this junk.

The biggest risk involved in using the Internet is that you will become a victim of online scams. There are more around than ever before. Fraudsters, often from Eastern Europe and Africa, harvest email addresses from the Internet or, in some cases, by hacking into company databases. Once they have created a suitably convincing email they send it to hundreds, even thousands of addresses at once. Some people unwittingly provide them with personal details such as a credit card number or password; they then raid their accounts.

Many have also been ripped off by e-bay auctions. They see something for sale and bid for it, but never get the goods. In May 2005 a Welsh teenager was sent to a detention centre for a year because he had advertised products he didn't have, including mobile phones, cameras, and computer equipment. Once the auction had closed, the victims were contacted and told that they had won. He usually asked them for cash to be placed into a bank account, which they would not see again. Calls would be ignored or he made excuses: meantime, he spent the money on designer clothes and weekends in New York, where he hired stretch limousines. Cardiff Crown Court heard that he taunted some of his deceived customers, and told them: "This is my business – I make people fools."

The Government says that scams are costing British consumers more than £1 billion a year. AOL, the Internet services provider, has published some useful tips.

• Use a Spam filter to block unsolicited emails before they reach you.

• Set up a separate email address for visiting public areas on the Internet, such as chat rooms and message boards.

• Use firewall software to protect your computer or home network against unauthorised access while you are online.

• Be careful about what you download, especially if you have any doubts about the source.

• Never give out personal information. If you are unsure about something, contact the company the email purports to have come from or log-on to its official website. Report suspect emails to your service provider.

• Use Parental Controls so that you can decide which websites your children access, who they can email, and even how long they spend online. Don't let them visit dodgy websites.

All this makes sense, but many of us are unaware of the dangers or can't be bothered to take the necessary steps. The jargon, and technology, can be daunting.

When I was the editor of a healthcare magazine I became particularly concerned about some of the medical advice on the Internet. Alongside the reputable sites were many others that were seriously misleading. Charlatans were peddling all sorts of miracle cures. It still happens. Some sites advocate suicide, give advice on methods, and discourage individuals from seeking psychiatric help, dismissing it as useless. Others promote drugs that have not been properly evaluated or ones that are counterfeit or contaminated. There is an awful lot of rubbish out there.

My teenage grandchildren think I'm a dinosaur because I like to write letters. I'm not alone in this: millions of our fellow citizens do the same. A well-written letter delivered through the postal service (called snail-mail by some) is best if one wants to say "this is important" or "this is really personal". Job applications should not be composed in haste and emailed to potential employers, who are quite likely to treat it as junk. Typing is acceptable, but make a point of reviewing carefully everything you write. It includes the spelling – mistakes stand out and make a bad impression. Handwriting has come to be regarded as old-fashioned but is still appreciated if you want to express sympathy or thank someone for a gift.

Classic writing paper is unlined (lined smacks of schoolroom). Avoid coloured borders, wiggly edges, and frivolous drawings unless you are corresponding with a friend or relative. A postcard is ideal for a brief note. Whatever you do, be sure to get the other person's name right. Fail in that, in a letter or email and you will annoy the recipient and look slipshod. The British will forgive many things but this isn't one of them.

Having It Out

English is so widely taught abroad that most immigrants arrive with at least some knowledge of the language. The same cannot be said of Welsh or Gaelic, which even the English find incomprehensible. Don't worry: you are not expected to speak all three.

The main problem is that many foreign teachers are not familiar with the words and expressions in use today, or with the concept of political correctness. Phrasebooks, too, tend to be behind the times.

When I first came to Britain, equipped with the English I had learned in a German school, I was often baffled by the idioms I encountered. I did not, for example, know what to make of words like dogsbody and posh, or what people meant when they talked about facing the music, kicking the bucket, living cheek by jowl, eating humble pie, cradle-snatching, reading between the lines, and having it out. I was also mystified by expressions like all mouth and trousers, head over heels, hard-boiled, giving the boot, big cheese, chisel, up to scratch, mud in your eye, and the bee's knees. None of this made sense.

Since then the language has been influenced by imports from America and other countries. Hollywood films and TV sitcoms have led to the widespread use of expressions like cool, chill out, gimme a break, in your face, go for it, and to die for. Asian 'yoof-speak' has also made a contribution with Hindi words such as gora and pukka and slang like 'innit'. Experts predict an explosive impact of the lingo used by the offspring of immigrants. "This will be an increasing trend", says the editor-in-chief of Collins Dictionaries. "If new words are used enough they will end up in the dictionary, and once they are there they will become English words too".

The business world has a separate language, which you will have to learn if you want a career in corporate management or in financial services. Your superiors will be impressed if you know what is meant by downsizing, delayering, re-engineering, profit margins, rights issues, flotation, maturity, hedging, and the bottom line. A careful study of business magazines and the financial pages of national newspapers should keep you informed of the latest buzz-words. The basic principle is never to use a simple word or phrase if you can find a complex one. Shops are retail outlets, tables are dinette units, the poor are 'lower socio-economic strata, and talking to colleagues in a meeting is 'qualitative, quantitative interfacing'.

You should also seek to become proficient in the use of euphemisms – the substitution of a mild or vague expression for a harsh or blunt one. Companies don't sack people – they 'let them go' or 'set them free to meet new challenges'.

Euphemisms are increasingly used in everyday conversations. Take sex. Most of us don't care for vulgar words like 'fucking' and have adopted a range of alternatives – sleep with, shag, boff, bang, tumble, score, getting your leg over, run around with, have a fling, and so on. Your genitalia are called private parts. (The penis is your manhood, member, or willy. If it's large you are well-endowed). Men who masturbate are taking themselves in hand, jerking off, wank, or doing a wrist-job. Gay, which used to mean cheerful, has replaced odd, queer, and pouff. A bastard is a 'love-child'.

Some people still tend to use old-fashioned terms like defending your virtue (a woman refusing to have sex outside marriage) and doing the right thing. (Marrying the woman you have impregnated). Mothers advise daughters to keep their legs crossed and not allow boyfriends to 'take liberties'.

Special care is needed in referring to a sexually attractive female. It is no longer permissible to use words like dish, smasher, and dolly bird. Men who make unwanted attempts to fondle women other than their wives are said to have 'hand trouble' and may be charged with sexual harassment – a serious offence in the eyes of the law.

This brings me to the thorny issue of what it is, and is not, politically correct. As noted earlier in this book (see Free Speech) it has become very important to understand the boundaries. You ignore them at your peril.

We are in territory of some complexity here, but the basic point is plain enough: you must watch your language, not only in matters like sex but also in anything to do with race or religion. There is, nowadays, a linguistic apartheid in which some people have a monopoly over certain words: blacks can say nigger or coon, and Bangladeshis can say Paki, but an Anglo-Saxon Englishman is not allowed to cross the line.

John Denham, then a Home Office minister, made the mistake of using the phrase 'nitty-gritty' during a police conference in 2002. A constable got up and said he would have faced a disciplinary charge for using the expression, which, it had been claimed, referred to the detritus at the bottom of 18th century slaveships. The officer later said he had also been advised not to refer to any of his colleagues as a 'good egg' because the phrase was allegedly taken from 'egg and spoon', which rhymes with coon.

Police forces, universities, local authorities and others have drawn up guidelines which together form an elaborate code on how not to cause offence over race, gender, disability, religion, and sexual orientation. The English National Opera has cautioned its staff against calling each other 'darling' (a common practice in showbiz) because it may be construed as sexual harassment. Judges have been issued with an Equal Treatment Handbook that lays down strict rules. It bans West Indian as having colonial overtones and mixed race as perojative. Coloured is condemned as an offensive term that should never be used, and oriental should be avoided 'because it is imprecise and may be considered racist'. Job descriptions such as postman, chairman, and fireman must be replaced by 'non-sexist' equivalents. 'British' should be used only in an inclusive sense, to cover all citizens of whatever background, and not as a synonym for white, English, or Christian. Even 'common sense' is deemed problematical, because it implies a value judgement.

An Italian friend of mine, who came to Britain in 2003, says that he wasn't told about any of this in his English class. He is puzzled by many words and expressions because the teacher never mentioned them. It is a common complaint. The obvious solution is to ask for an explanation, but many foreigners are reluctant to do so because they don't want to seem ignorant or risk being laughed at. The trouble is that, as a result, they are liable to misinterpret what is being said and find themselves in embarrassing situations.

Immigrants who seek to become British citizens, or who have already acquired that privilege, are expected to make every effort to understand what we are talking about. Few of us are prepared to admit that even people who were born in Britain sometimes have a problem. Londoners, for example, tend to find it difficult to communicate with Scots. The Scots, in turn, are often baffled by London slang. In between there is 'the north', which has its own lingo. People say "any road", instead of anyway, and "ay up, I'm feeling champion today".

When health authorities in Yorkshire recruited seven Austrian GP's to combat staff shortages they asked all doctors in the area to contribute to a glossary of local words they encounter at work. It included 14 different words for male private parts plus several for parts of the female anatomy such as 'melons' and 'boobs' (breasts). The Austrians were equally grateful for translations of phrases like 'chuck up' (vomiting), 'feeling queer' (off colour), 'clock' (face) and 'popped his clogs' (dead).

My friend gave me a list of words and phrases which he still finds confusing. I have selected a few, and translated them, which he (and you) will need to become familiar with.

Bugger. The dictionary says it means sodomite, but the word has many other uses. We shout "bugger" when something goes wrong (like hitting your thumb with a hammer instead of the bloody nail) and tell people to "bugger off" when they annoy us. We also use the word to admit defeat ("we're buggered") or to describe how we feel when we are tired and exhausted ("I'm buggered"). If something costs 'bugger all' it means that it costs nothing.

Belt up. This is another way of saying "shut up". People who waffle (talk on and on about nothing) may also be told to "put a sock in it".

Dog's dinner. My friend was surprised when I explained that the phrase means making a real mess of something. He had naturally assumed that it meant feeding his labrador with the tasty stuff he had seen advertised on TV.

Grub. When a colleague invited him to lunch, and said that the chosen restaurant had 'marvellous grub', he consulted his dictionary and found that it meant 'larva of insect, caterpillar, maggot'. He declined because he had no intention of eating such disgusting creatures. He now knows that the word simply means good food.

Her Majesty's Pleasure. This one really caught his imagination when he saw it in a newspaper. He was disappointed when I said that it was a legal term for putting someone in prison with no release date. I have no idea why it should give her pleasure.

Not my cup of tea. A common saying which has nothing to do with the choice of beverage, but means something not to your liking. If, for example, you are invited to an orgy, and don't fancy the idea, you should say that "It's not my cup of tea".

Loo. This is the proper term to use if you are invited to dinner by a middle-class couple and have to 'answer a call of nature'. Always ask where the loo is. Working class people say toilet.

Banger. The good old British sausage. It can also mean a cheap old car.

Gutted. If someone is really upset by something, like failing an exam or seeing England's cricket team beaten by the Australians, he may say that he is gutted. Young people seem especially fond of this word.

Blow me. Not, as some people think, a request to perform a sexual act. It is simply an expression of surprise.

Pissed. This is a vulgar way of saying that you have had too much to drink. Many people go to the pub, or to a party, with the intention of getting pissed. It should not be confused with the expression "pissed off", which means that you are angry about something.

Pillock. If you are called a pillock it means that you have done something stupid. Another mildly insulting term is prat. Ignore both unless you want to get into a fight.

Pull. To be on the pull means trying to persuade someone to have sex with you. Pulling seems to work best in discos and at parties. Do not, however, make the mistake of saying that you are looking for willing 'birds' – a term for young women that many regard as offensive.

Get stuffed. This is a crude way of telling someone who has annoyed you to go away. Many working class people prefer to say "fuck off", which means the same thing. New citizens would be well advised to use more polite phrases, like "please leave me alone".

Smashing. The dictionary says that to smash something is to break it utterly to pieces. Many foreigners therefore find it hard to understand why the Brits use the word as a compliment. To us, smashing means terrific.

Dodger. A dodger is someone who evades a task, like washing up after dinner or changing nappies. 'Dodgy' means that someone, or something, is not to be trusted.

On the house. Anything distributed free of charge, courtesy of the management, is said to be 'on the house'. Some people prefer to call it a freebie.

Fishy. Any situation that includes suspicious elements. A former Prime Minister, Benjamin Disraeli, is usually credited with inventing the term. The odour of fish, he said, made him think of doubtful political deals.

Moonlighting. Night affords lots of opportunities to take on a second job, usually part time. People who do this, often without the knowledge of their main employer, are said to be moonlighters.

Full of beans. This expression is said to have its origins in the practise of feeding horses on beans: it was believed to make them more energetic. It is commonly used to describe any unusually zestful person, but the idea that eating beans will result in boundless energy is a myth.

Off the wall. When we say that something is off the wall we mean that we think it's absurd, like a weird painting or a ridiculous plan. It may also be called 'off-beat', which sounds less aggressive.

Cock up. My friend assumed that it was a request from a member of the opposite sex. Not so: it means that, like him, you have made a mistake.

The English language clearly has many pitfalls. Getting things wrong will piss off your fellow citizens.

How To Pull Legs

Political correctness has also put significant curbs on humour. Many of us are fond of a custom known as 'pulling someone's leg'. This has no connection with medicine or torture but is a form of banter which we consider to be uniquely British. It involves making a mild and subtly disguised joke at another person's expense, and should not be attempted without training because there is a strong risk that you will be misunderstood.

The English have long claimed that they invented humour. William Hazlitt, writing in the 18th century, maintained that it could be traced to their intellectual mediocrity. "Now it appears to me", he said, "that the English are (or were) just at that mean point between intelligence and obtuseness, which must produce the most abundant and happiest crop of humour. Absurdity and singularity glide over the French mind without jarring or jostling with it; or they evaporate with levity. With the Italians they are lost in indolence and pleasure".

The charge of mediocrity would nowadays be regarded as close to libel, but most English people are convinced that they have a superior sense of humour. The Scots and Irish disagree: they point out that the Goon Show was created by an Irishman, Spike Milligan, and that Scotland's Billy Connelly is the funniest man in Britain. These are deep waters and I advise you not to take sides until you have learned to cope with the currents. Pulling the legs of the Scots, Irish or Welsh is a dangerous pastime for any Englishman and particularly hazardous for an immigrant who has not yet decided which nation in the United Kingdom merits his or her allegiance.

What is not disputed, except abroad, is that the *British* are better at humour than everyone else. There was widespread astonishment when

I was appointed the editor of *Punch* at a time when the magazine was still regarded as a 'unique British institution'. How could a German, of all people, be expected to know what was funny? I said that an editor was like the conductor of an orchestra: his job was to make the best use of talented contributors. As a naturalised citizen, I could bring a different perspective to the task. I did both for nearly ten years.

Let me offer some brief guidelines based on my own experience and observations.

There is more to humour than an ability to tell jokes.

You can steal narrative jokes from books and television, or from conversations you have overheard in a pub, but don't assume that others will find them amusing. They have probably heard them before and may find them offensive, especially if you mock their beliefs. Avoid anything that is blunt, sexist or vulgar.

Laugh at yourself.

The safest course is to make fun of your own shortcomings. A talent for self-deprecation is greatly valued: it shows that you don't take yourself too seriously. At the wider level, it explains the enduring popularity of TV series like *Dad's Army, Fawlty Towers,* and *Are You Being Served?*

The trouble with this type of humour is that people from other cultures tend to take it at face value. They assume that you have a poor opinion of your abilities and that the British are as inept as the characters they see on TV. It should be made clear, therefore, that self-deprecation is intended to convey the appearance of modesty. We don't really mean it, but regard it as preferable to boasting – though, of course, we have much to boast about. What foreigners fail to understand is our fondness for irony. They often complain that they never know when we are being serious or not.

The British like to think that they are particularly good at using humour in adversity. Indeed, this is said to be central to their character. We laugh, or at least smile, in circumstances where others would curse or cry – not because we don't recognise the gravity of the situation but because we want to demonstrate that adversity can be overcome by laughter. (A classic example is the bit in one of the Monty Python films where a knight keeps laughing as his opponent chops off his arms and legs).

It's OK to be silly.

A great deal of humour is concerned with childish themes, like practical jokes and bodily functions. We also like slapstick comedy: Charlie Chaplin and Benny Hill were British. But what makes us truly different (or so we like to believe) is our infatuation with nonsensical humour. The most famous exponents are Lewis Carroll, Edward Lear, and Spike Milligan. Read *Alice in Wonderland*, or listen to recordings of the *Goon Show*, and you will get a good idea of what this is all about.

Childishness is central to nonsense humour because it turns everything upside down and refuses to obey the rules of grown-ups. It is, in essence, a rebellion against the authority of orderly thinking and has the advantage of not being seen as a threat.

As a first-generation immigrant I was enchanted by the bizarre adventures of Alice and by the tales of Winnie the Pooh, Piglet, and Eeyore. The Goons were brilliantly nonsensical and, like everyone else,

I enjoyed the juvenile antics of *Monty Python's Flying Circus* and the silly *Carry On* films.

One British tradition which has remained hugely popular is the pantomime. Millions of us go to see a 'panto' every Christmas because we (and the kids) love a bit of old-fashioned tomfoolery. The shows have familiar titles like Aladdin, Jack and the Beanstalk, Snow White, and Sleeping Beauty but they are very different from the Disney versions. They are full of cheeky jokes. Some are risque and toe-curling but the groans are as much part of the pleasure as the laughs. The best also have imaginative sets that explode with glitter and gaudy colour, original music, special effects, and celebrities who welcome the chance to be silly.

The favourite character is a pantomime dame called Widow Twanky. 'She' is always played by a man, pretending to be a woman. (The principal boy, in turn, is usually a female). It is, however, more than a drag act. John Inman, the gay shop assistant in '*Are You Being Served?*' says that "it's a walk and a wig and a frock and an attitude; you have got your head around those and the character unfolds". Wyn Calvin, another actor who has played the dame many times, says that "you must fail to be feminine. You must attempt but fail; that's why it's funny to the kids".

Many stars of serious theatre, films, and television long to have a go. When Sir Ian McKellan was invited to play the widow in Aladdin he accepted at once because, he told journalists, "I have wanted to do this for 40 years. I loved panto as a child: it's the first form of theatre that children experience, so we must do it properly. The dame is a complicated character to play, but even so it's not the far from Shakespeare. There's soliloquy and direct address to the audience, there's spectacle, transformation, rude jokes and cross-dressing. I think I'll manage". The production at the Hackney Empire was everything that panto fans could desire, with riotous support from comedy policemen, tap-dancing pandas, vengeful undead Egyptian mummies, an airborne Genie of the Lamp, and even an impressive elephant.

There is a long-established element of audience participation in panto. "Look behind you!" everyone shouts when the villain creeps up on his unsuspecting victim. And when an actor makes some preposterous statement the collective response is supposed to be "Oh no, it isn't!" Half the audience will then bellow "Oh yes, it is!." (Much like our parliament really).

If you have never seen a pantomime, take your children to one next Christmas – it will give you a better understanding of what many of us mean by a British sense of humour. Don't get upset by some of the jokes: they are not aimed at you, or 'ethnic minorities' but are about pulling the legs of everyone, regardless of colour, sex, or religion. It may not last, because there are plans to bring in new laws which will make it a crime to offend our fellow citizens. If they are passed, judges will have the solemn duty of ruling whether comedians (and Widow Twanky) should join the burglars, drug dealers, muggers, and killers that overload our prisons.

Politicians are a legitimate target.

We are, thank God, still permitted to make fun of politicians. It is a British tradition which has survived the censorship imposed in so many other areas. Our leaders are constantly ridiculed by parliamentary sketch writers, cartoonists, and stand-up comedians. Few dare to complain because they don't want the public to think that they have no sense of humour.

Only the British, however, can play this entertaining game. Foreigners are expected to stick to mocking their own rulers.

Bah, Humbug!

There is a domestic version of the pantomime, in which dad pretends to be a cheerful old man with a white beard, dressed up in red suit and bellowing "ho ho ho". The idea is to make the kids believe that he has just come from the North Pole on a sledge pulled by reindeers so that he can distribute presents. Most children above the age of five know this is nonsense but go along with it because they don't want to disappoint their parents.

Americans claim to have invented Father Christmas. It isn't true, but they did come up with the silly suit and the "ho ho ho". A German, Prince Albert, introduced another popular feature – the Christmas tree – when he came to Britain and married Queen Victoria.

Neither has anything to do with religion. The same goes for office parties, silly paper hats, turkeys and mince pies, tinsel, and Boxing Day. There are carol singers and school nativity plays, but for most of us it's all about having a good time. This is why many people now call it 'Xmas'.

Giving presents is vital if you don't want to be compared to Ebenezer Scrooge, the Victorian miser immortalised by Charles Dickens in one of his novels. Scrooge famously dismissed Christmas as 'humbug' but changed his mind when the ghost of his former partner said that he had better start to be generous if he didn't want to spend eternity in chains.

Many people say that Christmas has become 'too commercial'. They are right, but it wouldn't have happened if we were not so eager to co-operate. Much time and effort is devoted to finding a 'suitable gift'.

It's not hard if one is shopping for something the kids would like, because they generally make their wishes known well in advance – often by writing a letter to Father Christmas and making sure that Mum and Dad see it before it goes off to the North Pole. The big problem for adults is what to buy for each other, which involves having to deal with tricky questions like '*how generous should we be?*'

There are a few basic rules to keep in mind. Don't forget to remove the label or sticker before you start wrapping. Never tell the recipient what you have paid: it's frightfully vulgar. And if you are given something you hate, like a gaudy tie or pink slippers, the proper British response is "Oh, great, this is what I always wanted".

The monarch traditionally addresses her subjects on Christmas Day. Queen Elizabeth has, in recent years, made a point of acknowledging that Britain has become a multicultural society. Her TV broadcast in 2004 included film from royal visits to a Sikh temple and a Muslim centre. She noted that "religion and culture are much in the news these days, usually as a source of difference and conflict, rather than for bringing people together". The Queen went on: "Discrimination still exists. Some people feel that their own beliefs are being threatened. Some are unhappy about unfamiliar cultures. They all need to be reassured that there is so much to be gained by reaching out to others: that diversity is a needed strength, and not a threat".

There are other celebrations, such as the Hindu Divali, the Jewish Hannukah, Chinese New Year, and the Christian Easter. The Scots have Hogmanay, which many regard primarily as an excuse to drink themselves into a stupor. We also have rites which are of pagan origin and are celebrated in various forms in many cultures around the world.

Easter commemorates Christ's resurrection, but the name is a variant of Eostre, the saxon Goddess of spring, and customs like giving eggs are based on pagan fertility rites.

Valentine's Day, February 14, is intended to show that we British know how to be romantic. It is a time for chocolate covered cherries, flowers, mushy cards, candlelight dinners, or underwear emblazoned with hearts. Newspapers are full of inane messages like 'Eeyore loves Piglet'.

Valentine's Day began as the Roman fertility festival of Lupercalia, an erotic knees-up during which young bachelors would draw the name of teenage girls from a lottery. Whoever they picked would be their sexual partner for the rest of the year. The Christian Church roundly condemned such pagan practices but introduced a sanitised version in 498 AD. Valentine was a priest martyred in the third century. Some legends say that he was executed for defying an edict against marriages for Roman soldiers, whom the emperor believed would fight better without family ties. In one account he fell in love with his jailer's daughter and wrote a poignant goodbye letter 'from your Valentine'.

Hallow'en is a descendant of All Soul's Eve, a festival of communion with the dead, another pagan ritual. Children love it because it gives *them* an opportunity to put on fancy dress. You are expected to give them a 'treat', even if they are complete strangers who knock on your door while you are watching *Coronation Street*.

Bonfire Night was originally a 'fire festival' welcoming the winter. As I mentioned in a previous chapter, it was adapted (in the seventeenth century) to commemorate the defeat of a plot to blow up the Houses of Parliament. Some people still burn an effigy of the ring leader, Guy

Fawkes, but it is now mainly another excuse to have a party – often with elaborate fireworks – which may go on for several days rather than just on the night of November 5th.

There are also calendrical events which were invented by entrepreneurs in their quest to squeeze as much money as possible out of a spendthrift populace, such as Mother's Day and Father's Day. We even have a Red Nose Day, which has a more laudable objective – to raise funds for charity. (You are encouraged to buy and wear a plastic red nose, to show that you have the twin virtues of generosity and a sense of humour).

The whole business is vulgar, sentimental, and mercenary. You may well be tempted to say "bah humbug". You are under no obligation to take part, but many of us feel that the rituals, traditional or contrived, make life more fun, and, at the same time, remind us of the obligations and affections which we all too easily forget or take for granted.

Why, Oh Why?

It is often said, usually by foreigners, that the British don't like to complain. This isn't true.

Our newspapers complain about everything – the government, Brussels, the French and Germans, immigration, the National Health Service, football managers, the BBC, banks, insurance companies, the railways, tourist 'hordes', the Post Office, the Archbishop of Canterbury, the royals, the behaviour of rock stars, and much else. Radio and TV producers make scathing programmes about hooliganism, perverts, estate agents, tour operators, smokers, carmakers, and what builders are doing to our countryside. It's known as why, oh why? journalism.

We also have an assortment of 'community leaders' who constantly bitch about racial prejudice – real or imagined – and about the welfare system, the police, local councils, and the media. Trade unions bang on about fat cats, working conditions, lay-offs, and the inadequacy of the minimum wage. Politicians who belong to opposition parties complain about everything that ministers say or do.

It is true, however, that many of us prefer to *moan*, which isn't the same thing. Moaning is a low murmur rather than an aggressive (and public) expression of discontent. We say 'not again' if our train is late and 'typical' when traffic lights break down or a warden slaps a ticket on our car seconds after the time on the meter has expired. This is usually accompanied by a shrug, because we understand that nothing can or will be done about the problem we are moaning about.

We hate to make a fuss, so even our complaints tend to be understated. We use phrases like "that's not fair" or "that's not nice". Offenders may be told "I don't think much of that" or "do you mind not doing that?" We may also dilute our criticism with a hedge – as in "I don't want to be rude, but..."

Some people write a letter to the *Times* or the *Daily Telegraph*, drawing attention to a grievance and pointing out that "it is not a British way of doing things". (How, you may wonder, are they so sure? Best not to complain: new citizens are expected to keep a low profile).

A fundamental rule is that 'ordinary people' must always show proper respect for authority. Attempts to bully officials are invariably counter-productive. You are more likely to get results if you use phrases like "may I ask you", "would it be possible", "I think you ought to know", or "I'm sorry to bother you, but..."

Brits who like to think that they are the 'better sort' sometimes resort to rather crude gambits. Here are a few examples:

"I am a personal friend of the chairman / minister / mayor".

This blatant attempt to intimidate others frequently turns out to be a bluff. Don't even think of making such a claim unless you are certain that he or she will back you up. Powerful people tend to get very annoyed if someone they have never heard of, or may have met once at a cocktail party, use their name to scare subordinates.

"You will hear from my lawyer in the morning".

This, too, is probably a bluff. Most of us have second thoughts about involving a lawyer once we have calmed down, partly because of the cost but also because it seldom does much good. He or she may write

WHY, OH WHY?

a strongly-worded letter, and get an equally forceful reply from another lawyer, but that will generally be the end of the matter unless you are prepared to embark on a long and expensive battle in the courts.

"I am taking this up with my MP".

We *all* have the right to do so, and it's certainly cheaper, but the threat is unlikely to impress civil servants in Whitehall, who know how to deal with MP's (send a polite letter, but don't do anything) or corporate executives, who take the view that politicians should not seek to interfere in the private sector.

"My son works for the Daily Mail".

This gambit is intended to show that one has clout with the press, and that there will be embarrassing publicity. It *may* work if he can convince the editor that the complaint is about something that can be called a 'scandal' or involves someone who is a celebrity. It will *not* work if you have an argument with your neighbour – too trivial – or with the Inland Revenue. (Even bold editors don't like to offend tax inspectors, who may decide to investigate their own behaviour).

"My uncle / brother / godfather / cousin will sort you out".

A working class threat which is illegal, and un-British, but not one that can be ignored or brushed aside because, regrettably, some of our fellow citizens feel that their complaints need to be backed by muscle. Keep in mind though, that some of us also have tough relatives or can afford to employ what in middle class circles is known as 'rough trade'.

175

This brings me back to my earlier point – moaning is acceptable and therapeutic. It may not get you anywhere, but you won't make serious enemies or raise your blood pressure to a level which, your doctor will tell you, is more likely to lead to a premature departure from the country which is now your home than an angry and relentless campaign to defeat people who have upset you.

A Nation of Gossips

Here is another myth: the British don't like to gossip. The truth is that we *love* it.

Forget what you may have heard about our alleged obsession with privacy and reluctance to 'wash dirty linen in public'. One of the most popular features in national newspapers is the gossip column: a daily compendium of tittle-tattle about the royals, politicians, actors, pop stars, TV chefs, footballers, and other 'celebrities'. The magazine *Private Eye* specialises in washing dirty linen. Many of us also exchange gossip on the Internet.

The usual excuse is that we have a right to know what prominent people are up to. This is fair enough if they are breaking the law (or, in the case of politicians, abusing their power) but most gossip is about their private life. What we really want to know is who is doing what with whom.

The stories are often embellished, to make them more titillating. When, for example, the press disclosed that David Mellor (then a Cabinet Minister) had an affair with a Spanish actress we were told that he always wore the shirt of his favourite football club when he made love. It was a lie. Mellor resigned and later became a journalist himself. (Columnists can have as many affairs as they like without having to worry that they will lose their job).

Many showbiz people don't mind what the press says about their sex life. They share the view expressed by Oscar Wilde in one of his plays: "there is only one thing worse than being talked about, and that is not being talked about." (Wilde came to regret his fondness for publicity. A homosexual affair led to a battle in court and he ended up in jail). Some celebrities, eager to stay in the public eye, feed the press with stories about their sexual adventures. They may or may not be true; what matters is that they invariably attract extensive coverage.

Rumours may also be invented with the aim of undermining a rival. The victim can issue a denial, and even threaten to sue (if he or she can discover the source) but readers tend to believe in the old adage that there is no smoke without fire.

Another motive may be to make money in the stock market. The City is a notorious rumour factory and shares can rise sharply when some story gets around; the inventor then sells before it turns out to be false.

A former Prime Minister, the late Harold Wilson, was furious when speculators spread rumours about sterling. He accused them of 'selling Britain short' and warned that they would 'pay a heavy price.' He went on to quote Don Basilio in Rossini's opera, the Barber of Seville:

A well-timed insinuation

A suggested intimation

Half denying, half implying

O'er the town will soon be flying

Expectation, fear and wonder

Gathering strength like distant thunder

E'er increasing, never ceasing

Is to new invention spurred.

The speculators were proved wrong at the time, but two years later the pound was devalued.

Dinner party gossip tends to be mainly about celebrities. It's a form of social bonding. But it may also be malicious gossip about a neighbour, acquaintance, or colleague at work. This can easily lead to trouble, so there are some unwritten rules you need to keep in mind.

Talking behind someone's back creates hard feelings.

Never gossip about someone you know personally because there is a strong chance that he or she will get to hear about it. Many relationships are seriously damaged by indiscretion. Why take the risk?

People who gossip about others will also gossip about you.

Never reveal anything about yourself that could be used against you. It may be tempting to boast that you have found a clever way to dodge taxes, or to jump the NHS queue, or to gain some other advantage, but don't assume that it will remain a secret. You certainly can't rely on the discretion of strangers you meet at a party or in a pub.

If you learn that people have talked about you behind your back, confront them. They may deny it, or claim to have been misquoted, but they will be more cautious in future.

Beware of people who say "don't tell anyone, but..."

Many gossips pretend that you are the only person they are sharing their secret with. The aim is to make you feel privileged, but you are unlikely to be the first person they have talked to. They *expect* you to blab.

Don't participate in gossip.

If others gossip about people you know make it plain that you don't approve. At the very least, refuse to participate. (Americans have a useful phrase: "I don't want to go there"). Try to change the subject.

Defend your friends.

If someone is bitchy about a friend say that you find it offensive and threaten to tell him or her about it. Your friend will appreciate your loyalty and do the same for you.

All this is common sense. Pass it on.

Under The Doctor

Another allegation that needs to be challenged is that we are a nation of hypochondriacs. The British, it's said, spend too much time worrying about imaginary ailments.

I doubt if we are worse than the French or Italians, but I certainly know people who fret about every twinge. Doctors warn that it can lead to 'hypochondriasis' – defined as 'the unrealistic belief or fear that one is suffering from a serious illness, despite medical reassurance'. They say that it's often based on a misinterpretation of normal bodily functions, such as gurgling in the abdomen or bloating, which is normal as fluids move through the intestinal tract.

Doctors must share the blame. They use so much scary jargon. There is, for example, a condition they call Seasonal Affective Disorder Syndrome. What it means, in plain English, is that many of us get depressed by the grey, wet, dark, miserable British winter. Another is known as a 'phobic disorder', which is said to be an irrational fear of a specific object or situation. Examples include heights, confined spaces, storms, flying, injections, mice, snakes and spiders. 'Social phobia' is persistent fear of being exposed to the scrutiny of others, causing intense anxiety and sometimes a panic attack. You may also have heard of 'white coat hypertension' – elevated blood pressure when visiting the surgery of a doctor or dentist.

Hypochondriacs have a strong urge to discuss their state of health with anyone who is willing to listen. They boast about being 'under the doctor', which is intended to make us feel that they deserve our sympathy. They also love pills, many of which can be bought over the counter in supermarkets. They take all kinds of supplements and hoard remedies for every possible illness. They constantly seek medical advice and get angry if they are told that there is nothing wrong with them: the GP, they insist, has somehow failed to find the underlying disease.

Not surprisingly, doctors have little patience with all this. They resent the fact that their competence is questioned, and they don't want to waste time that should be devoted to patients with genuine problems.

There are, of course, worries that cannot be easily dismissed. A good doctor will always give careful consideration to symptoms and decide what, if anything, needs to be done. But most GP's can only give an average of ten minutes to each patient, which may not be enough to ensure a correct diagnosis. It is tempting to prescribe a pill and tell us to get plenty of rest. If they are not sure, they may order tests or refer the patient to a specialist. It can be alarming but usually happens in order to eliminate possible causes.

Some of my friends in the medical profession say that the 'nation of hypochondriacs' label is unjust. They claim that it would be more accurate to call Britain 'a nation of wimps'. Many of us, it seems, will put off seeing a doctor until our symptoms are severe. This is particularly true of men. Statistics show that they are half as likely to go to their GP as women. Even when they do venture into a surgery, 40 per cent of the appointments have been made by their wives or girlfriends.

This has led me to a personal reflection: am I a wimp? The embarrassing answer is "probably yes". I am not a hypochondriac, but whenever I am urged to see a doctor I usually say "Oh no, I don't want to bother him".

Like many other British men, I tend to regard illness as a sign of weakness.

I have this macho idea that I can handle everything that life throws at me. There must be a pill that can solve the problem without running off to a surgery where I have to face female receptionists and nurses who want to play mother.

A report published by Men's Health Forum says that we take more risks throughout our life than women. We are more likely to be overweight, drink too much, and generally fail to take proper care. If we have a medical problem we want to get it 'fixed' in the same way that we take our car to the garage. Women tend to be more aware of what can go wrong, which no doubt explains why they have a longer life expectancy.

We tend to make all kinds of excuses. Being 'too busy' is one of them. We postpone or cancel appointments because we have 'more important things to do'. The real reason is that we fear that the doctor may give us bad news. When we finally make the effort, and are told that there is indeed a serious problem, we curse ourselves for not seeking help early enough.

A growing number of people – men and women – are turning to 'alternative medicine', which is based on holistic principles. It aims to deal with the patient as a whole, not merely with physical symptoms. Practitioners say they take into account not only the body but also the mind and spirit. It appeals to hypochondriacs and wimps because they want to believe that there is a better way. Some of the remedies, such as acupuncture and Chinese herbal medicine, have been introduced by immigrants.

Doctors acknowledge that complementary medicine (a term they prefer) can play a useful role but warn that it can raise false hopes and expectations. No reputable therapist, they say, would claim to have a cure for life-threatening diseases like cancer and heart disease. What concerns them is that patients may risk missed or delayed diagnosis, or that they may stop or refuse effective conventional treatment. They also stress that, contrary to popular belief, alternative medicine isn't always safe. Some remedies are dangerous and many practitioners lack proper qualifications.

Politicians like Gordon Brown claim that our National Health Service embodies 'the best of Britain'. Many people, especially those who are having to wait months for an operation, feel that if this is the best the country can do, we *really* have reason to be worried.

Britain At Work

It is sometimes said, usually by Americans, that we are not serious about work. This isn't true, but many of us would like to see it done by others – especially if it involves menial tasks like collecting rubbish and digging up roads. We feel that our proper role is that of manager or supervisor.

The perception that the British are indolent is due, in part, to a factor I have mentioned before – films and TV series about the upper class. But the main reason why so many Americans misjudge us is that they don't understand the difference in our cultures. We don't accept that, as one of their billionaires famously claimed, "work is more fun than fun". (He should try collecting rubbish). Middle class Brits dislike their pushy, let's-do-it-now approach to business and the working class is less willing to be exploited by ruthless employers.

Much of the criticism is outdated. We work longer hours, these days, than our European neighbours – and, for that matter, many Americans. This is not because we have become workaholics – though we have our share of them – but because we need the money. Taxes have gone up and so has the cost of living. (We are not just talking about grocery bills here, but also about mortgage repayments and essentials like a new car and holidays abroad).

Another crucial point is that immigration has forced us to be more competitive. This was not an issue thirty or forty years ago because most immigrants, especially those from Asia, were glad to settle for whatever job they could get. We could rely on them to do the dirty work. But they, too, now want to be managers or supervisors. Many of the *are*.

An obvious solution is to welcome more people from countries like Albania, Poland, and Latvia. This became government policy when they joined the European Union. We are not sure where it will lead to, but it should ensure an adequate supply of cheap labour for the next few years.

As a new citizen you will already be familiar with British attitudes. There are, however, some immigrants who clearly have not yet learned what is expected from them and who are puzzled by our rules and expressions. Here are the answers to some of the questions you may be asked:

What do the British mean when they say "don't work too hard?"

This is intended to be a warning. Excessive zeal is unpopular because others feel obliged to display the same enthusiasm if they want to keep their job. Trade unions have gone to a great deal of trouble to ensure that Britain has laws against it.

We are, however, prepared to make exceptions. If you are self-employed, the rule does not apply. A plumber or electrician, for example, is expected to work *very* hard. This also goes for newsagents, owners of pubs, and others who run a small family business.

What is the 'black economy'?

This has nothing to do with racism but refers to a sector of the economy in which people like plumbers, electricians, painters, and gardeners insist on being paid in cash so that they can dodge taxes. The Inland Revenue is hot on their trail and you should not assume that you will get away with the practice: tax inspectors are allowed to be zealots.

What is meant by the 'north-south divide'?

Economists use the term to describe regional differences in prosperity. London and other areas in the south have seen dynamic growth. The northern regions, and the Midlands, have been left behind. The Government has tried to fill the gap by expanding the public sector, but this is expected to become more difficult in future. Forecasters predict a sharp widening of the divide in the coming years. The message is obvious: your chances of getting (and keeping) a job are best if you live in the south.

Why don't the British like salesmen?

Some of us still take a snobbish view of 'trade', but attitudes have changed because there is now a greater emphasis on services than on manufacturing. Most of us are selling something: financial advice, an idea, a philosophy, or just ourselves. What we don't like is aggressive American-style salesmanship. We are suspicious of salesmen who try too hard, the kind of people who won't take no for an answer and who get visibly annoyed when the customer walks away.

We also don't like to haggle. It may be standard practice in the country you have come from, but it is not the British way of doing business – unless, that is, you are working on a BIG DEAL (more about this later).

Why are some people called 'fat cats'?

Because they are 'greedy'. Fat cats head large corporations and get an 'indecent' amount of money for their work. They are under constant attack from the media, trade unions, and left-wing politicians. It is, however, OK to be greedy if you are a footballer, pop star, television presenter, fashion designer, or newspaper editor.

What is a 'golden handshake'?

A payment, also known as a 'golden hallo', made to people who had to be persuaded to reject tempting offers from others. Once onboard, they may be fitted with 'golden handcuffs' (a package of benefits) to prevent them from leaving. If the appointment turns out to be a mistake, and the company decides to terminate the contract, they may be entitled to a 'golden parachute' – they can bail out with another cheque in their pocket.

The bad news is that ordinary workers don't qualify for such generous treatment. You have to be a corporate superman or a City high-flier.

What can I do about racial prejudice?

It depends on what form it takes. You have a strong case if it leads to racial discrimination. Britain has even more laws against that than against excessive zeal. Indeed, we have a concept called 'positive discrimination', which means that you get preferential treatment. It doesn't apply to *white* working class males – the last group it is possible to demonise without breaking the rules of racial etiquette.

What is the 'glass ceiling'?

This is a term invented by feminists who complain that they are barred from boardrooms and therefore denied the opportunity to become fat cats. Once a woman reaches a certain management level, they say, she hits a 'glass ceiling'. Many insist that the complaint is no longer justified because a growing number of top jobs have gone to women. It is, however, true that the majority of fat cats are male.

Laws banning sexual discrimination in the workplace were introduced many years ago, but women often find it difficult to prove that they have failed to get promotion because of their gender. Employers usually claim that a male candidate had better qualifications.

Here too, 'positive discrimination' is said to be an appropriate way to deal with prejudice. Many women who have reached the top disagree – they prefer to show that they have got there on merit.

What will happen in the years ahead, I predict, is that men will bitch about the unfair behaviour of female bosses.

Why are so many employers unwilling to give jobs to older people?

Because they are still stuck in old ways of thinking. Youth has been worshipped for so long that they can't see that times have changed. Average life expectancy in Britain has increased dramatically and people over 50 can look forward to many more productive years. They tend to be more reliable, conscientious, and loyal than young workers. Yet they are usually the first to be sacked when companies embark on their periodic bouts of downsizing and delayering. many find it hard to get another job.

Ageism, which affects both sexes, is universal. Well, *almost*. Chairmen and chief executives – the fat cats who do all that downsizing and delayering – play by different rules. They consider themselves to be perfectly capable of running large organisations in their 60's and even 70's.

The good news is that age discrimination is due to be made illegal by October 2006. There are also plans to change the mandatory retirement ages. But laws are not much good if they are not enforced and if they leave loopholes. As with racism and sexism, you may still find it hard to prove that you have been rejected or sacked because of your age.

What Britain really needs is a change of culture. It may happen for a practical reason. Economists predict that the 25 to 34 age group, which employers currently covet, will decline by 20 per cent during the next two decades. By contrast, the number of 55 to 64 year-olds is expected to rise by 50 per cent. It is a trend that companies will not be able to ignore.

Meanwhile, of course, you could simply *lie* about your age.

An Ageing Country

The prime minister likes to portray Britain as a 'young country', but that is no longer true. A third of us (including Blair himself) are over 50. A quarter of all women are over 60 – an age group that outnumbers children under 16. The demographic centre of gravity is shifting from youth to the later years.

What is true is that our media, fashion, music, and advertising industries glorify the young. They are seen as vigorous, daring, sexy, fun. The 'old' are depicted as frail, staid, and tight with what little money that have. They are patronised, mocked, bossed around, snubbed, treated like children and simpletons, and otherwise humiliated.

Disdain breeds outright discrimination. Healthcare for older people, especially in hospital, is often lamentable. They are widely regarded as a nuisance, a waste of time and money. The British Institute of Human Rights says they are "routinely treated with a lack of dignity and respect that simply would not be accepted in relation to other social groups".

All this tends to come as a shock to new immigrants who were told that the British are polite, tolerant, and helpful.

When we reach the point where we are labelled 'senior citizens' we get lumped together in stereotype images: the grumpy old man, the granny tottering along the high street with her zimmer frame, the tiresome pensioner who keeps banging on about the war. Youth is idolised: 'senior citizens' are relegated to the walk-in bath, chairlift, Dad's Army zone of life.

Women tend to be more affected by this negative attitude than men because of the widely held belief that their best days are over at an even earlier age. Many dread the prospect of turning 40. It isn't hard to see why. Magazines, advertisements, and fashion shows all feature stick-thin models who are barely out of their teens and who are clearly thought to represent all that is admirable in a woman, even if they can't string two sentences together. "Middle age is more terrifying than it has ever been", one insecure female columnist wrote in *The Independent* recently.

It's utter cobblers when you look around you. Women in their 40s are often far more attractive (even to young men) than the skinny kids who strut around the catwalk in camouflage pants, tank tops, tiny tube-like dresses, and other preposterous outfits created by publicity-hungry designers.

Not long ago, you may recall, eleven middle-aged members of a Yorkshire Women's Institute took their clothes off for a charity calendar, in a defiant attempt that the advancing years had not robbed them of their appeal. There were the usual jokes and patronising comments, but the calendar was a smash hit. A film based on their effort, starring the delicious Helen Mirren and Julie Walters, was also a big success. I hope that it persuaded many other women that middle-aged need not be 'terrifying'.

One of the many myths perpetuated by the media is that older people are no longer interested in sex, or have lost the ability to perform. They go on endlessly about the sexual exploits of the young but dare not fly in the face of the convention that says " no sex, please, we're pensioners".

The truth is that many of us enjoy it more than when we were young, inexperienced, and hasty. We tend to be better lovers because we are more considerate. (Find out for yourself if you don't believe me). We are also less likely to contract, and pass on, a sexually transmitted disease than the careless, bed-hopping young rabbits. Doctors say that people in the 18-24 age group are at greatest risk.

Beneath the myths lies the erroneous assumption that older people all think, act, and look much the same. In reality there is no age group more varied in physical abilities, personal styles, tastes, desires and financial status. Yes, many of us are frail, staid, struggling to make ends meet. But there is also a whole generation of 'baby boomers' (born between 1945 and 1960) who are fit, active, and well-off.

Research by SAGA, a company often mocked by the media despite its impressive commercial success, has established that the over 50s have 80 per cent of all private wealth and a 30 per cent higher disposable income than the under 50s. There are 20 million of us and we collectively spend more than £215 billion a year. Yet retailers and the advertising agencies who devise their campaigns still prefer to focus on the young, who have much less purchasing clout. What they fail to understand is that the baby boomers are different from their parents and grandparents. They grew up in a relatively affluent era and are used to a better lifestyle, which they are determined to maintain. They are less concerned with passing an inheritance on to their children than previous generations.

As Britain ages, retailers and others will have to make a greater effort to meet their needs and wishes. They should start by learning what they are.

The over 50s don't think of themselves as 'old'; they think of themselves as people. Many of us don't want to be referred to by age at all. Marketeers may find it convenient to use neat categories, but that is a foolish approach. We don't walk into stores and ask if they have products for men and women over 50. We don't like advertisements that depict us as has-beens walking hand-in-hand towards the sunset. We know what we want and are not easily seduced by hype and slick salesmanship.

Average life expectancy in Britain has risen by three decades since Victorian times. It is now at least 76 for a man and 80 for a woman. The over-85 year olds are the fastest growing age group in our population. More of us are growing older than ever before.

This isn't a 'blip' but a trend that is expected to continue. Some scientists predict that life expectancy will double by 2050 because of further dramatic advances in medicine. It may seem fanciful, but so did the optimistic forecasts their predecessors made a century ago.

We should certainly redefine what we mean by terms like middle-age, elderly and old. Does 60 seem old? Not to me. How about 70 or 75? Many people of that age group play golf or tennis; some run in marathons. Sir Francis Chichester made the first solo sailing trip around the world at 65. Nelson Mandela became president of South Africa at 75 and got married again at 80. Picasso continued to paint right up to his death at 93, and PG Wodehouse was still writing funny novels at 90. The Queen is in her late 70s but doesn't plan to retire. If one enjoys good health, age is a state of mind.

Surveys on both sides of the Atlantic have sought to discover what alternative terms are preferred by people over 60. 'Elderly' was found to be the label they disliked most, followed by 'golden oldies'. A third said they didn't object to being called 'seniors' but that they would rather be thought of as 'mature adults'. So would I. But it doesn't much matter what label is used if attitudes remain unchanged. The media has a vested interest in this. Most newspapers have an ageing readership and mature adults make up a high percentage of radio and TV audiences. They don't want to be ignored or cordoned off as if they live in another planet. Politicians, too have good reason for taking a more enlightened view: we tend to make greater use of our vote than the young. The over-50s will increasingly set the political agenda and determine the outcome of elections.

The 'Time Bomb'

The prospect of living even longer than their parents should please the young, especially as they stand a better chance of doing so in good health. We have already seen a vast increase in both the range and the effectiveness of drugs; this has been combined with major improvements in surgery, helped by an impressive array of new technology. The decoding of the human genome, or 'book of life', is expected to lead to another revolution in medicine. Scientists say that by 2050, and quite possibly before, they will have conquered diseases like Alzheimer's, cancer, diabetes and arthritis.

It seems extraordinary, therefore, that longevity is more often seen as a problem rather than a blessing.

You may have heard or read about the so called 'demographic time bomb'. This has become a fashionable term for what some economists claim will be the big issue of the 21st century. (I referred to it in 'Bonking for Britain'). You may well think that terrorism, and the possibility that we will all be terminated by a nuclear bomb, is more serious threat but they prefer to focus on the economic troubles we allegedly face because of our ageing population.

Their case is that the 'elderly' are bringing down the welfare state and threatening Britain's economic future. As their numbers rise, the cost of healthcare and pensions will 'explode'. A shrinking number of young workers will have to shoulder a growing burden and at some stage there will be an age war – an acrimonious conflict that will divide the country and set generation against generation for decades to come.

There are several things wrong with this alarming thesis. Firstly, it assumes that we are all dependent on state support. The statistics I mentioned earlier show that many people over 50 can afford to make their own arrangements. A lot of us are already doing so – recent years have seen substantial growth in private healthcare and personal pension schemes. They also pay taxes and will continue to pay providing they are given the opportunity to go on working. It is perverse to whinge about the 'burden' and, at the same time, seek to shove them out of the workforce as soon as possible. The young cannot have it both ways.

Secondly, the argument ignores the fact that many dependent people are not elderly. They include numerous young adults and we do not refer to them as a burden. Many are unemployed, for one reason or another, and it would be politically incorrect to call them anything more damning then unfortunate. Mature adults are quite right to object to the misconception that they, and they alone, are a 'drain on resources', especially as they have helped to finance the system for so many years. It is certainly unfair to blame them for the rising cost of the National Health Service. They make considerable demands, but the same is true of numerous young men and women.

I noted in an earlier chapter that obesity among children has become a real menace. So has the self-indulgent lifestyle of many young adults. Booze, smoking, 'recreational drugs' and other bad habits destroy the body as surely as anything to do with the ageing process. The demands on the NHS are swamping the system because so many people court ill-health through their own stupidity. The 'elderly' tend to be more aware of the risks and, therefore, take better care of themselves.

Thirdly, we *could* have more young workers if we welcomed more immigrants instead of complaining that there are already too many of them.

There is a more fundamental point: why should we see the issue in terms of young versus old? Many young people are also affluent enough, these days, to look after themselves and their children. They should be encouraged to save, so that they won't have to rely on the state in years to come. It isn't happening on any significant scale. Surveys have found that nine out of ten of those aged 18 to 35 know that they need to save but have no interest in it. They want everything now and prefer to run up debts. Many are counting on inheritances that they may never get because the money that would have once been passed on to the next generation will, of necessity, be spent in the later years of a long life. (Even if some should be left over, the Inland Revenue will grab up to 50 per cent).

If there is an age war, we will want to be on the winning side. But what form is the conflict supposed to take? Rebellions, these days, tend to be led by students and trade unions but a battle against pensioners is unlikely to attract public sympathy and they can't expect much help from politicians, who are too scared of losing the votes of the fastest-growing sector of the electorate.

Ministers say they are concerned about future generations, but this is a dubious claim. Governments seldom look beyond the next general election, so they usually come up with quick fixes. There is an endless stream of pledges, vows, targets, mission statements and other eye-catching gimmicks which never add up to anything with shape or vision. The 'time bomb' is a long term problem, so why worry about it *now?*

Economists say that it will have to be addressed in the near future and have come up with various proposals. One, predictably, is to 'soak the rich'. A previous Labour government did that, but came to regret it. The Chancellor of the day, Denis Healey, found that inflation had pushed many Labour supporters into tax brackets hitherto reserved for 'the rich'. They didn't like it. Some left the country. Others hired accountants and lawyers who were experts in legitimate tax avoidance. Many decided that it was pointless to work hard, or run the risk of starting a business, if most of their income and profits were hijacked by the Treasury. The current Chancellor, Gordon Brown, also believes in the 'redistribution of wealth' but if he goes too far we could see a repeat of what happened in the 1960s and 70s.

Another proposal is that young couples should be encouraged to have more children by offering them a bribe. This has already been tried in Italy, with little success.

A more sensible solution would be to stop spending such vast sums on maintaining a bloated bureaucracy and on expensive military adventures abroad. (Getting rid of Saddam Hussein cost billions). Politicians should also make it clear that there are limits to what we can expect the state to do for us. Too many people demand 'funding' for what they insist are worthy causes, without giving much thought to where the money is supposed to come from. What we need to accept is that compassion has to be tempered with realism, and that in future we will have to take greater responsibility for our own welfare. There is a simple term for it: common sense.

How To Get Rich

The

MONEY

PROGRAMME

My next guests both began their long careers working newspaper rounds.

It obviously helps to be wealthy. Millionaires don't have to worry about ageism at work or claim welfare benefits. You may find it strange, therefore, that many of our fellow citizens say that they have no desire to be rich. "Money doesn't buy happiness", they insist.

The expression is often used by people who know that they are unlikely to make any serious money unless they hit the jackpot in the national lottery. They console themselves with the thought that the rich are miserable. It is a ridiculous assumption. *Some* are unhappy but not because they are loaded. There are other reasons: poor health, troublesome relationships, or the inability to come to terms with the fact that they are not immortal.

Let's be honest. Money may not guarantee happiness but it can buy a lot of good times. It can also buy other things: attention, respect, flattery, and a wide range of services. It can certainly help one to be miserable in comfort. Many of us would like to be rich so that we can find out for ourselves.

When I came to Britain as a teenage immigrant I was poor and *longed* to be wealthy. What mattered to me above all was freedom of choice: the ability to decide what kind of work I wanted to do and where to do it; freedom from dependence or handouts; freedom to travel or to do nothing at all if I didn't feel like it.

I accept that one doesn't necessarily need a fortune to feel free. But I have never found anything good to say for poverty.

The truth is that many of the people who show such disdain for money, at least in public, are hypocrites. They want to be wealthy but are unwilling to make the effort required to get there. It is the dream of instant, easy millions that makes the national lottery so popular.

The odds against turning that dream into reality are astronomical. There are better ways, and we will come to them in a moment, but let me ask first: do *you* want to be rich? If so, how ambitious are you? Would a million be enough? How about two or three million? Or do you just want to be affluent enough to live well and to not be a 'burden' to anyone if you reach the age of 80 or 90?

Britain has more millionaires than ever before. It is no longer an exclusive club: the membership includes pop stars, footballers, fashion designers and models, chefs, car dealers, actors, TV personalities, and even authors.

Many of today's super-rich are immigrants. Jasminder Singh came to this country from Kenya in 1970 and has made a fortune in the hotel business. Simon Halabi, born in Syria but now a British citizen, owns shopping centres in Slough and Stockport; he is reckoned to be worth £500 million. Tony Mascolo didn't speak a word of English when he came over from Italy and became a hairdresser in his father's salon; he and his brother Guy now have more than 350 salons worldwide. David Shamoon left Iran after the fall of the Shah in 1979 and settled in London; he has since made £100 million in shipping and hotels.

A million still seems a huge sum to most of us, but keep in mind that it isn't what it used to be because of inflation. My generation is painfully familiar with this great deceiver. Inflation (a fall in the value of money due to rising prices) creates an illusion of wealth. People think that they are better off than they really are. Who knows what a million will buy 20 years from now?

OK, it's still a nice cushion to have. So let's consider some of the ways in which you can get hold of it.

Marry a fortune

This is the path traditionally chosen by younger members of the British upper classes. Having a title helps but isn't important unless your target is an American. Essential qualifications are social skills and knowing 'the right sort of people'. You also need to be able to devote plenty of time to the chase, which isn't easy if one has to earn a living. Many families provide their offspring with a generous allowance so that they can take a year off and do it in style.

There is no age limit: indeed, older people are often more successful because the seriously rich, particularly widows, tend to feel more at ease with someone of their own age. And you don't have to confine yourself to Britain. You may fare better in the US, which has more multi-millionaires than any other country. Make sure, though, that the money isn't tied up in a trust fund or that you are not expected to sign a prenuptial agreement.

Be kind to wealthy relatives

This is another upper class tradition. Aunts and uncles used to consider it their duty to 'remember' younger members of the family in their will. It could be anything from a silver tea pot to a million. The practice is less common than in the past, but there will always be relatives who are a soft touch if one is kind to them. Sadly, many young people can't be bothered to make the effort. They are dismayed to find, when the will is read, that the money they had been counting on has been left to charity.

If you have wealthy relatives don't forget to send flowers on their birthdays, visit them as often as you can, and offer to help in some way, especially if they are disabled. (It is, however, bad form to make it obvious that you are only doing it because you hope for a financial reward.)

Aim to be a corporate fat cat

I said, earlier on, that people who have reached the top of the corporate ladder are widely accused of being 'greedy' – a charge not made in the case of pop stars and footballers. Some chief executives earn more than a million *a year*, but so do many showbiz celebrities.

The trick here is to convince institutional shareholders – the City – that you are the best man or woman for the job. It helps to have a reputation for ruthless cost-cutting. Make sure that your service contract includes perks like bonuses, share options, a big pension, and lavish compensation if you are fired.

Start your own business

Many immigrants start their own business – this is what I did myself. There is much to be said for independence, but you need to understand some basic rules.

A common error is to lease or buy a shop, pub, or restaurant and then to do all the work yourself. It may seem like a good idea, but it won't make you rich. You are more likely to get a heart attack. A *chain* of shops or restaurants can be run by managers, leaving you with ample time for holidays in the South of France. The ultimate objective should be to sell part or all of the company for millions.

This, of course, involves taking risks. All ventures do – even marriage. You took a risk when you decided to make a new life in Britain. But it's not the same as gambling. Successful entrepreneurs have a vision and a realistic business plan. They calculate the upside and downside of everything they do. If an idea isn't working they cut their losses and move on to the next one.

Some people maintain that success is all a matter of luck. It isn't true. What they call 'luck' generally turns out to be the ability to recognise opportunities when they arise and make the most of them. Their mistake is to find some reason for not doing so. They tell themselves that the risks are too great. When others have a go, and get rich, they are much envied. So here is the second rule: you can make your own luck.

You will obviously need capital. It doesn't have to be your own, and you don't necessarily have to rely on help from your bank. There are other sources of finance. 'Venture capitalists', for example, specialise in putting up money in return for a share stake. They are more patient than bank managers: their motive is to make a substantial profit on their investment within five or six years. If all goes well, your company can 'go public', which involves selling shares via the stock market. Or you can sell the business to a larger group and spend the rest of your life playing golf. Both sides win.

Andrew Lloyd Webber, whose musicals have made him super-rich, once told me that when he started in show business he found it hard to get backing. His break came when he heard of a list of 'angels' circulating in London's theatreland. Angels are people who, like venture capitalists, are willing to take risks because they want a share of the action. Many, he said, were doctors and dentists. Without their support, his early musicals might never have seen the light of day.

You may also be able to find an investor who has faith in your talent and project. It is worth asking relatives, friends, or contacts if they know anyone who might be interested in your venture.

Sometimes an offer of financial support can come out of the blue. This is what happened to David Lloyd, the tennis player. When he played the professional circuit, he travelled to parts of the world where tennis clubs were popular. He decided, when he left the pro game, to launch a club in Britain. He found a piece of land near London's airport, invested all the money he had earned from tennis, and tried to raise more capital. The banks were negative: he kept knocking on doors to no avail. Then, one day, someone he had never met called him and said: "Look, I've got money to invest. I love tennis". By the mid 1990s he had a chain of 13 clubs, with an annual turnover of £25 million, and was able to float the company on the stock market. He later sold his shares to Whitbread, the brewers, in a deal that netted him £20 million. The angel also made a handsome profit.

Play the property game

Many of us like to brag about the fortune we have made by investing in property with the help of other people's money – usually a mortgage. This is still widely believed to be one of the best ways to get rich.

The housing market has certainly seen spectacular gains, but the popular view that 'you can't lose' is a myth. In the early 1990s, national average house prices *fell* by 20 per cent and they did not return to their previous peak until eight years later. Such downturns may not matter if you don't have to sell. You can just sit tight and wait for a recovery. But what if you should run into financial problems and can no longer meet the mortgage payments? This is what happened to many people. They had to sell their home for less than what they paid for it, and in some cases for less than the amount they borrowed. The experience was also painful for speculators who bought several properties in the hope of making easy profits.

Could it happen again? Sure it could. I have no doubt that the housing market will do well in the long run, but there are bound to be periodic downturns and they may be more marked, and last longer, than you had bargained for.

The property game has its own set of rules and it clearly pays to be familiar with them.

Don't buy if there has already been a prolonged boom and everyone tells you that it will go on and on. The best time to make your move is when the music stops.

Don't make commitments you may come to regret. Borrowing a large sum of money may seem like a good idea when interest rates are low but they could go up – in the early 1990s they reached a peak of 15 per cent. Be realistic about what you can afford. *Be careful* in your choice of location. There is a reason why property in some areas is cheap: the people who are selling no longer want to live there. Look for up-and-coming areas and try to find a neglected house or flat that is worth doing up.

Play the stock market

Many people have also made (and lost) a fortune in the stock market. Trading in shares has several advantages. You don't need a lot of capital to start, deals can be done more quickly than in the property game, and you can spread your risk by buying shares in different companies. But similar rules apply. What goes up can come down, often with alarming speed.

Nowhere is advice more plentiful than in financial services. You'll soon become aware of the wide variety of people who are eager to handle your money and take their slice off the top. Some are little more than salesmen who recommend shares because they want to generate commission. Ask yourself why, if they are so clever, they work for a living. It would surely be far easier to trade on their own account, as angels do. The short answer is that most of them are not nearly as good as they would like you to think they are.

Many of us are tempted by what we believe to be hot tips. They are usually based on nothing more than a rumour. Genuine inside information is hard to come by – and you may end up in jail if you act on it.

As with property, playing the stock market requires good timing. Don't follow the crowd and don't be greedy. (There is an old Wall Street axiom: the bulls make money, the bears make money, but the pigs get slaughtered). Remember that, until one sells, a paper profit is just that. It may evaporate if one hangs on too long. It is irritating to get out and then see the price go up, but it is even more irritating to stay in and watch it dropping like a stone. The great Nathan Rothschild famously said that he had made his fortune by always selling too soon. His formula was: "sell, regret – and grow rich".

Room For More?

Migrationwatch, a so-called 'think tank', predicts that Britain's population will swell by at least six million over the next thirty years. Nearly one in ten of the extra numbers, it says, will be migrants and their families. The proportion of ethnic minorities looks set to grow to twenty per cent, or one in five.

The Shadow Home Secretary, David Davis, claims that immigration could fill six new cities the size of Birmingham within the next three decades and 'endanger the values that we in Britain rightly treasure'. He wants it halted 'before it is too late'.

All this is guesswork. The precision is bogus. We don't *know* what will happen because so many things could change. A future government may decide to withdraw from the European Union and, by doing so, deny people from other EU states the right to settle in this country. The EU may change its rules. An economic depression may make Britain less alluring. Many more of us, including disillusioned migrants, may seek to start a new life abroad. But we all know why right-wing politicians try to alarm us with their predictions: they want the vote of Brits who see immigration as a problem, not as a benefit.

The Labour Government takes the more sensible view that we need immigrants to keep the economy growing. It accepts the need for some controls (indeed, they are already in place) but points out that simply closing the doors to new arrivals is not a realistic option or in Britain's best interests. The Home Secretary says there is plenty of room for more. This is certainly true of Scotland. It has the highest rate of population decline in Europe and by 2009 the number of people living there is expected to fall below five million. The First Minister says that reversing this trend is the single biggest challenge facing the country. Professor Robert Wright of Sterling University reckons that Scotland needs to attract 50,000 immigrants a year. The Scottish Executive, which has launched an initiative known as Fresh Talent, wants to offer potential newcomers a home if they fail criteria for entering England.

One of the most corrosive causes of anti-immigrant feeling is the idea that, far from adding to the economy, they live off the state. They are said to be 'scboungers' who only came here because we provide generous 'handouts'. This may be true of some, but Home Office studies have shown that the majority contribute more to public finances than they take out.

Immigrants have usually been a source of prosperity and new vitality in countries where they have settled. Imagine Britain today without its Asians and their ethos of hard work, respect for education, family loyalty, and determination to succeed. They, and refugees, have been responsible not only for transforming whole areas of British life but in some instances ensured their survival. (Where would the NHS be without Asian doctors and nurses?). Many were born and brought up in this country and are as British as Michael Howard, who is the son of Jewish immigrants from Eastern Europe. Yet they are all too often seen as an alien presence because their skin isn't 'white'.

Opposition to immigration, however unattractive its expression, is rooted in human nature. It springs from fears, both rational and irrational. Individuals are unsettled by the changes to the familiar contours of their community which migrants bring. They are worried about the shared cultural assumptions which underpin social cohesion. At its heart, the debate is not about economics but about race and ethnic diversity.

Much has been said and written about the hostility towards Islam. The Commission on British Muslims and Islamophobia claims that it permeates every part of our society. This is an exaggeration, but there is no doubt that attitudes have been greatly influenced by sporadic acts of terrorism, notably in America, and much-publicised calls by radical clerics for a 'holy war' against the west. Many non-Muslims fear that there is a plot to turn Britain into an Islamic country. This is certainly the aim of the extremist organisations, but we need to keep a sense of perspective. Muslims comprise less than 3 per cent of the population and most are moderate, peaceful, and law-abiding citizens. They have a visible attachment to their religion and the customs associated with it, but they are not interested in political involvement and deplore the rhetoric of the fanatics.

The Muslim Council of Britain has repeatedly condemned terrorism and urged Muslims to co-operate with the police. Talk of a 'clash of civilisations' merely helps the agitators. I am not a Muslim, but one of the main reasons why I decided to become a British citizen, all those years ago, was that people were free to choose their own religion. There are other faiths, such as Hinduism and Judaism, and Britain has managed to accommodate them all because most of us want harmony, not conflict.

It is perfectly valid to say to immigrants: "we are glad to have you, and we will respect your culture and beliefs, but it was your choice to come to this country. By making it, you accepted your responsibility to integrate". It is equally valid for immigrants to say: "thank you, but please make it easier for us to do so".

A common complaint is that ethnic minorities live in enclaves, instead of seeking to become part of the mainstream of our culture. This is undoubtedly true, but we should ask ourselves why we have this form of apartheid. An obvious reason is that many newcomers feel more comfortable in an environment that has familiar features, but it is also true that many of us don't want them to integrate and therefore make little effort to help.

Britishness has always been a work in progress. Immigrants and their children have made us all think a little harder about what exactly it means to be British. What is extraordinary about this country is the extent to which we have retained a sense of common identity, even as we have watched the nature of change before our eyes. It's difficult to define that identity, but it is still there.

This book has, I hope, provided some helpful guidance, but, inevitably, many people will disagree with it. There is certainly ample scope for argument but I think we can agree on one fundamental point: tolerance, respect for each other, and an open mind are 'the values which we in Britain richly treasure'.

How Good Are You?

Test your ability to integrate by answering this quiz. Check your answers and rating with the chart at the end.

1. Which of the following statements is wrong?

a) The royal family's official name is Windsor.

b) The Prime Minister is the head of state.

c) Guy Fawkes tried to blow up parliament.

d) Catholics are excluded from succeeding to the British monarchy.

2. The national football team from your country of birth plays against England. Would you:

a) Hope that England will lose and cheer if it does.

b) Learn the words of Rule Britannia.

c) Express dismay if England wins.

d) Say that "it's only a game".

3. Who, or what is Hogmanay?

a) An unusual type of pig.

b) A British rock band.

c) A village in Suffolk.

d) New Year's Eve in Scotland.

4. Which historic event is known as 'The Battle of Britain?'

a) The last war between the Scots and the English.

b) Race riots in Liverpool.

c) A showdown between British and German pilots during the second world war.

d) Margaret Thatcher's stand against the miners.

5. You are in a queue and someone pushes his way past you. Would you:

a) Call him a bloody moron.

b) Break ranks and try to get ahead of him.

c) Shrug your shoulders and stay in line.

d) Say, "excuse me, but I was here before you".

6. What is the 'special relationship?'

a) A happy marriage.

b) Britain's close ties with America.

c) A homosexual relationship.

d) A friendly understanding between the British and the French.

7. You are advised to eat humble pie. Would you:

a) Ask where you can buy it.

b) Try to find out the recipe.

c) Admit that you were wrong about something and apologise.

d) Say that you are a vegetarian.

8. Which of these statements is correct?

a) A British citizen is allowed to punish his wife physically as long as it's done in his own home.

b) You are entitled to shoot burglars.

c) Criminals are innocent until proved guilty in a court of law.

d) You can get away with anything if you offer a big enough bribe.

9. You are offered an OBE. Would you:

a) Ask what it is.

b) Find out how much it costs.

c) Point out that the British Empire no longer exists.

d) Say how much you are looking forward to meeting the Queen.

10. You are told that a friend has 'kicked the bucket'. Would you:

a) Admit that you don't know what it means.

b) Ask why he got mad with the bucket.

c) Wonder about his sanity.

d) Find out when the funeral is going to be.

11. How do you feel about cricket? Is it:

a) A boring sport.

b) An opportunity to see England humiliated by India or Pakistan.

c) The world's most civilised game.

d) The ultimate test of your ability to integrate.

Check your score.

Each correct answer scores one point.

1. Only b) is wrong. The Queen, not the prime minister, is head of state.

2. You should, of course, learn the words of Rule Britannia.

3. Hogmanay is New Year's Eve in Scotland – great if your liver can stand it and you can dance a reel.

4. The Battle of Britain was fought by British pilots, known as 'The Few', against the German Luftwaffe. They won.

5. "Excuse me, But I was here before you" is the traditional way of dealing with such un-British behaviour.

6. The term 'special relationship' is a term invented by the British to describe our close ties to the United States. Most Americans have never heard of it.

7. 'Eating humble pie' means coming down form a position you have assumed. You are expected to grovel.

8. The correct answer is c). We British try to be fair.

9. The OBE is an honour you should accept, even though we no longer have an Empire. The Queen will give you a nice medal.

10. 'Kicking the bucket' means to die. You should, of course, attend your friend's funeral.

11. If you live in England, the right answer is c). It does not apply in Scotland, Wales or Northern Ireland.

How did you get on?

Three points

Oh dear, this won't do at all. How on earth did you manage to become a British citizen?

Five points

Not bad, but you had better do some more homework.

Eight points

Good. Many people who were born in Britain would find it hard to beat your score.

Eleven points

Congratulations – you have hit the jackpot and are entitled to claim that you have what it takes to become fully integrated.

Appendix

The Home Office has published official guidelines for new citizens. Here are some of the key points.

As a British citizen, you have the 'right of abode' in the United Kingdom and are no longer subject to any form of immigration control. This applied equally to any of your family registered with you and to any children born to you from now on, unless for any reason they are not British citizens at birth.

This means that your previous indefinite leave to enter/remain, or settled status, no longer applies to you. If you wish to travel on a non-British passport, it must be endorsed to show that you have the right of abode. This is not the same as saying you are a British citizen.

The law allows you to retain any other nationality you may already hold. However, some countries do not allow dual nationality. If you were a national of a country which does not allow dual nationality, the authorities of that country may either regard you as having lost that nationality or may refuse to recognise your new status.

Suppose you have kept the other nationality and visit the country concerned. International law allows authorities to treat you while you are there as if that is your only nationality. The British representative there cannot give you assistance or protection against those authorities.

If you are planning a visit to the country of your old nationality, and you are not sure whether you have lost your old nationality, there is a way to find out. Before you travel ask the nearest Consulate or High

Commission for that country in the United Kingdom. If you have not lost the old nationality and you want to renounce it, send the letter or document to the Foreign and Commonwealth Office. It is evidence of your right to British protection while in that country.

Under the laws of some countries but not under British nationality law, a married person automatically has the partner's nationality and the children have a parent's nationality wherever they are born. So if your wife, husband, or child is visiting the country of your old nationality the advice in these guidelines applies to them too.

Another point to keep in mind is that we still have different categories. Information on how a British Overseas Territories citizen, a British Overseas citizen, British subject, British protected person or British national (Overseas) can become a British Citizen can be obtained from the Home Office or from a British Consular Office abroad.

Addresses:

Home Office IND

Immigration and Nationality Policy Directorate

3rd Floor, India Buildings, Liverpool L2 0QN

Telephone: 0151 237 5200

Foreign and Commonwealth Office

Nationality and Passport Section

Consular Division, Old Admiralty Building, London SW1A 2PA